Changing Kids' Games

Changing Kids' Games

G.S. Don Morris, PhD
California State Polytechnic University

Jim Stiehl, PhD
University of Northern Colorado

Human Kinetics Books
Champaign, Illinois

Library of Congress Cataloging-in-Publication Data

Morris, G.S. Don.
   Changing kids' games / G.S. Don Morris, Jim Stiehl.
      p. cm.
   Bibliography: p.
   ISBN 0-87322-187-7
   1. Physical education for children. 2. Games. 3. Movement
education. 4. Sports for children.   I. Stiehl, Jim. II. Title.
GV443.M66 1989
372.1'3–dc19   88-22097
                                                                CIP

Developmental Editor: Jan Progen, EdD
Production Director: Ernie Noa
Copyeditor: John Wentworth
Proofreader: Linda Siegel
Assistant Editors: Phaedra Hise, Valerie Hall, and Holly Gilly
Typesetter: Brad Colson
Text Design: Keith Blomberg
Text Layout: Denise Mueller, Denise Peters, and Jayne Clampitt
Illustrator: Ranee Rogers
Cover Design: Jack Davis
Cover Photo: Jim Corley
Printed By: Versa Press

ISBN: 0-87322-187-7

Printed in the United States of America

10 9 8 7 6 5 4 3 2 1

Human Kinetics Books
A Division of Human Kinetics Publishers, Inc.
Box 5076, Champaign, IL 61820
1-800-DIAL-HKP
1-800-334-3665 (in Illinois)

To the adventurous risk-takers who continue to seek new possibilities in games.

CONTENTS

LIST OF GAMES

BASIC MOVEMENT GAMES

Tag Games
Foot Tag or Pair Tag
Same Place Tag
Add-On Tag
Catch Me if You Can
Snipe-Snorp
Octopus Tag

Relay Games
Tractor Race
Take It Back
From Here to There
Keep It Together
Put It in the Mailbox
Hold On
Snake Along

Reception and Propulsion Games
Busy Bee
Keep Your Field Clean
10-Pass
The Boxer
Have a Seat

BALL GAMES

Invasion Games
Hit the Club
Bombs Away
Stop Me if You Can
On Target
Go-Bots on the Loose

Softball and Baseball Games
Three Flies Up
One Base
Maple Hill Ball
Figure-Eight Ball
Maple Hill—Hit and Go

Basketball Games
One on One
Pass and Shoot
Four Corner Relay
Pass and Turn
Basketbowl
Back-to-Back Basketball
Adapted Handball

NET GAMES

Volleyball Games
Keep It Going
Three Hits
Four Corners Volleyball
Air Ball

Tennis Games
Face to Face
Hit the Target
The Switch

Under-the-Net Games
Hit the Wall
Hit the Pin
Ball to Ball
All for You

ACTIVE ACADEMIC GAMES

Memory Games
One Behind
Couples Races

Math Games
All 4s Circle Math
The Number Grid

Language Communication Games
Design a Letter
Parts of Speech
Homonym Game

PREFACE

The childhood shows the man
As morning shows the day.
From *Paradise Regained*, John Milton

It is no secret. The ideas in this book originated not from lofty adult visions or abstractions, but from the tearful complaints of a little boy whose daddy and "uncle" were not including him in a backyard game of croquet. This pint-sized, cat-chasing whirlwind of noise and dust was not going to allow two adults to lock him out. Indeed, the adults were astonished by his persistence, as well as by his cleverness at "distorting" the game so all could play.

The boy's ability to adapt the game of croquet to his own needs made us realize how ingenious kids can be. The inquisitiveness, vitality, and imagination of children has always been apparent. They possess a natural inclination toward games, especially ones involving movement. Our attempt here is to capture what kids have taught us about games for players of *all* ages, and to offer you the possibilities they have shown us.

The book begins with our impressions of the purposes behind some particular games. We then discuss how to change games in ways that we and more than a thousand teachers, coaches, and students have found useful. Following these "how to" chapters, we share some games and game modifications that have been successfully gym-tested. We repeatedly urge you to add your own personal touches to the games as we have described them. We believe that the games you select, modify, or invent should fit your purposes, values, teaching styles, resources, and, of course, your players.

Our efforts in creating this book were supported by many people in many ways. We gratefully acknowledge the following colleagues for their support: Rainer Martens, Gwen Steigelman, and Jan Progen at Human Kinetics Publishing Company; the students and teachers at Maple Hill School in Diamond Bar, California, and at Newman Elementary School in Chino, California; our friends at Beitostolen, Norway; and Ranee Rogers, our illustrator.

Our closest support came from those with whom we share our dreams, our commitments, our joys . . . and our laundry: Kerry, Lori, Philip, Jennifer, Kari, and Peter, who is no longer a pint-sized kid.

PART I

PLANNING, DESIGNING, AND PRESENTING GAMES

This section of the book provides you with strategies for adapting known games and for creating new ones—games that use a wide range of materials and equipment and that are appropriate for all ages and abilities, in all kinds of places, and under a variety of circumstances. Although this book is primarily written for use with young people, the concepts are applicable to players of all ages. You will not likely find your favorite "already designed" game here; however, you will receive information that can lead you to create new favorites of your own design.

Experience has taught us that games leaders need not be familiar with a large number of games. We have found that many players thoroughly enjoy games that they know well and prefer to play them again and again rather than learn new ones. We have also found that many games described in various books are not approved by all players and thus require modification. Consequently, in this section of the book we encourage you to take the liberty of changing games that are familiar to you and also to invent new games especially fitted to your purposes and to your players.

The first chapter explores the nature of games and some possibilities available through games. In the ensuing chapters we offer a model for designing games programs, specific strategies for creating games, and suggestions for presenting games in a manner that will inspire enthusiastic participation by your players. As you read through these chapters, keep in mind that the games you and your players design will be limited by only your imaginations.

CHAPTER 1

WHY PLAY GAMES?

Games are popular not only in schools and recreation programs but in society at large. Witness our bookshelves (*Games People Play; Games for the Superintelligent; New Games; Video Games; Man, Play, and Games*), our films and television shows (The Only Game in Town, "The Dating Game," "The Newlywed Game"), and our language ("Don't play games with me!"), and one might easily surmise that Americans are preoccupied with games.

Games: A New Idea?

Although seemingly a contemporary phenomenon, people's interest in games can be traced back hundreds of years. Chess, for example, was a product of the Middle Ages and still enjoys considerable popularity. A type of football, mentioned long ago by Shakespeare in two of his plays, was banned by Edward II and other medieval kings because of danger to life and limb, but a variation of the game remains popular as rugby today. The "Spelling Bee," a favorite during the last century, is still with us today. And Parker Brothers' *Monopoly*, created in the 1930s, continues as one of our most popular board games. Indeed, the bibliography bearing on the historical, scientific, and educational aspects of play and games is enormous and demands a distinct scholarship of its own. Suffice it to say that games have been long appreciated and have captured the imagination of adults and children alike.

Games Are Fun, and Much More

We find it difficult to discuss games without first examining the closely related concept of play. It has been said that understanding the atom bomb is child's play compared to understanding child's play. Indeed, many scholars with diverse viewpoints have sought to understand the nature of play. Determining the point of intersection of all these diverse views is a difficult task. Nonetheless it is apparent that children left to their own devices will play (Eisen, 1988). So, in order to provide a frame of reference, we must define *play*, and then *games*.

Children seem to define themselves and their world through the modality of play. Consult any dictionary and you will likely find numerous definitions of the word play. We regard play as an enjoyable, serious, voluntary activity that the participants consider to be outside of the ordinary world.

Play is enjoyable because it is engaged in "for fun's sake," with little thought of the consequences. Play is serious because it provides opportunities for enhancing a child's feelings of mastery and for promoting his or her sense of being important. Play is unreal because players step out of reality and enter an imaginary world. Eating, writing a novel, and riding a motorcycle can be fun, serious, and voluntary, but they are not *play* because they are not apart from the real world. Play represents an arena that people enter to lose themselves—paradoxically, however, people sometimes find themselves through play.

Unlike play, *games* are usually structured and have more or less predictable outcomes. Participants play games with a certain goal in mind; they do not have the complete freedom to follow impulses and are more confined because behavior becomes subordinated to the anticipated goals (see Figure 1.1). In games, players place limitations on the play world and turn play into a contest. The limitations include

Figure 1.1 Games involve anticipated goals and predictable outcomes.

prescribed space and time boundaries, agreed upon rules, and clearly defined goals. Games are played with much energy and involvement; the more intense and serious the play, the more likely the rewards of success and fulfillment. Games, then, can be defined as "activities confined by implicit rules and in which there is a contest between players in order to produce predictable outcomes." In short, a *game* is a voluntary contest with agreed upon rules and clearly defined goals.

Though games may be considered contests, the important differences between games and other contests (such as professional sports, war, human relationships) are that

- games exist in a play modality (i.e., a step out of the real world);
- winning or losing is a short-lived condition relevant only to the game itself;
- games may be replayed with the same opponents; and
- games require cooperation by players in adhering to explicit rules and implicit game-play behaviors—in other words, fair play.

What Can Games Do?

Most teachers, coaches, recreation leaders, and parents want to contribute to the quality of young people's lives—their development, their achievements, and their overall well-being. One way of accomplishing this is through games. There is not universal agreement, however, on the value of games. Historically, games were often derogated as trivial and unimportant. Games are *fun*; hence, the reasoning goes, they are not legitimate activities, especially in schools. By way of contrast, some sports and physical activities have long been praised as sources of character building, delinquency reduction, and leadership development. Only recently have educators begun to recognize games as important tools for improving instruction.

We suggest that the value of a game lies in the purpose for which it is designed. Some games may be designed solely for their enjoyment. Others may have more serious purposes, such as fostering certain attitudes and values, presenting academic subject matter, promoting socially desirable behaviors, enhancing physical skills, or assisting in the development of personal attributes such as honesty, bravery, perseverance, and acceptance of self and others. Still, a most important feature of game playing is that participants enjoy themselves more when they are playing than when they are not. Whatever is acquired during game playing is acquired with pleasure.

Why Movement Games?

There are games of chance, games of strategy, games of physical skill, academic games, board games, party games, and even funeral games! Our emphasis in this book is on games that involve *movement*. That is not to say that each game will have movement as its primary focus. For many of the games we will describe, movement is incorporated solely as a motivator. For other games in this book, movement itself is the primary ingredient. No matter what role movement plays in a particular game, *all* of our games offer the players an opportunity to move.

By its very nature, movement is a powerful entity. It invites possibilities not readily available through other means (e.g., reading, watching movies, listening to tapes). First of all, movement can be fun and thereby add to the enjoyment of games. Games are fun; movement games are doubly fun. Most important, movement comes naturally to kids—which opens an exciting possibility: Through movement games we can con-

Figure 1.2 Movement games open exciting possibilities for everyone.

tribute to the development of children and, at the same time, rest assured that they are enjoying themselves (see Figure 1.2).

Activities involving movement afford unique opportunities and experiences. Through movement, for example, children can increase their potential for range and effectiveness of motion and for cardiovascular efficiency. They can also release tension, gain self-understanding, test prowess, learn teamwork, and simply derive pleasure from movement experiences. Thus, while children are learning movement games, they are at the same time improving themselves without realizing it.

Although movement and movement games can be easily justified from an academic standpoint, we also heed the more personal, emotionally appealing aspects of movement games. For example, one pleasant recollection is the joy of watching a group of kindergartners trying to balance on roller skates for the first time, their brows creased with concentration, their eyes intent with excitement. What fun it is to teach these little people, people to whom movement games are a

---

The fifth-grade students at Adamsville School had been modifying games for quite some time when Lenny first arrived. Today they happened to be playing a variation of kickball. Lenny had never played kickball. In fact, he had not played many games because most people agreed that a boy confined to a wheelchair could not participate in vigorous activities.

But this was a special class. The children immediately began to introduce themselves to Lenny and invited him to participate in the game. Lenny was frightened—he had been alone before, but never in this sense. This time he was alone in his belief that he could not participate in such a game. The other children were already embracing a "can do" spirit and were determined to include this newcomer.

Lenny was assigned to the team at bat, some members of which had been deciding on a strategy for including him in a manner commensurate with his abilities. Instead of kicking a ball and running bases, Lenny had to maneuver his wheelchair through some obstacles and then squirt a water pistol at a paper cup that was balanced on a traffic cone. If he could get to the cup, knock it over, and return home without colliding with any of the obstacles, he was pronounced "safe."

Sometimes he succeeded, and sometimes he did not. His classmates determined what he *could* do, verified their strategy with us, and then agreed that this was an acceptable option. Lenny was no longer merely a spectator. His was not a case of token involvement, but of genuine participation—of inclusion.

world of entertainment as well as a learning experience. Or the cerebral-palsied fifth grader who, after being self-absorbed for so long, was invited to play in a modified kickball game—and proved to be the star of the day. That single event provided an important breakthrough in this child's self-confidence, skill development, and willingness to develop friendships. It also served to remind us of the potential value of movement games.

Some Purposes of Movement Games

Games can be used to assist any child in reaching his or her maximum cognitive, social, emotional, and physical potential. What justifies the use of movement games is the unique contribution to each child's development. Although there is no common agreement regarding the nature and priority of game purposes, the following list typifies expectations of many people as they design and use games. It is our opinion that none of these goals need be selected at the exclusion of another.

Enhance Movement Skill Development.   Any popular game or sport requires movement skill. The skills may be complex, or they may

Figure 1.3   Movement games contribute to the development of movement skills.

be relatively simple or basic. To enjoy a variety of activities, children must learn basic skills such as running, jumping, turning, kicking, and throwing (see Figure 1.3). As they develop a repertoire of basic skills, they establish the efficiency, ability, and versatility necessary for playing and enjoying many of the activities valued in our culture. This is important not only during the school years, but also as the individual pursues leisure experiences in later life. The emergence of many movement skills is to some extent a matter of growth and development; but encouragement and instruction through movement games may be helpful if the child is to acquire or become proficient at more complicated skills.

Nurture Feelings of Self-Worth. By providing successful and meaningful movement-game experiences, we can contribute to a child's healthy attitude toward self and others. Research suggests that a child's self-image and confidence are likely to depend on how skilled he or she is at certain games and activities. In addition to promoting skill development, we can give children time and opportunity to be thoughtful about themselves and their relationships with others. They can be encouraged to express how they feel and to develop empathy for others. Children who can accept themselves and their physical capabilities are more likely to participate willingly and enthusiastically in sports and other physical activities. They are also more likely to engage in beneficial relationships with their teachers, coaches, parents, and peers.

Promote Physical Fitness. Research clearly shows that many physical and psychological diseases affecting adults stem from inactivity.

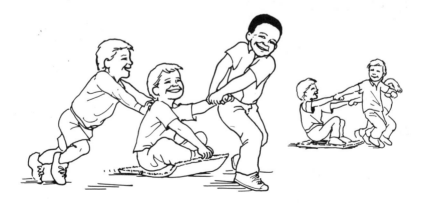

Figure 1.4 Movement games promote physical fitness.

Such conditions as high blood pressure, coronary heart disease, and obesity can be partially attributed to a sedentary lifestyle. In a more positive vein, dynamic vitality, productivity, and health in our adult population are commonly associated with youth fitness. Fit children are more likely to grow into fit and healthy adults. We have a unique opportunity through movement games to contribute to children's strength, power, flexibility, postural alignment, endurance, and body composition (see Figure 1.4). These games should include *all* children, as children of all ability levels will benefit from these offerings.

Foster Enjoyment and Satisfaction.   As previously mentioned, a prime ingredient in all movement games is enjoyment. Children enjoy participating in physical activity and find it personally satisfying. "Enjoyment," as used here, means more than simply "fun." To illustrate, a person may enjoy reading, or painting, or perhaps training for a marathon. In none of these cases must the enjoyment be simply an amusing diversion. On the contrary, enjoyment often involves discipline and hard work; consequently, it frequently results in personal fulfillment and an ongoing pursuit of excellence, especially if the activity continues to be challenging. In movement games we can foster personal satisfaction, enrichment, and a sense of "aliveness" through activities that are enjoyable and motivating. Moreover, we can embrace the child's active, playful spirit as a legitimate concern.

Figure 1.5 Movement games encourage the use of specific cognitive skills.

Invite Use of Cognitive Skills.   Children can learn how to learn, not simply how to perform. Through movement games and certain deliberate ways of presenting the games, children may participate in specific cognitive operations, such as comparing and contrasting, categorizing, hypothesizing, inventing, synthesizing, decision-making, identifying and solving problems, abstract thinking, and many more (see Figure 1.5). The ability to think for oneself contributes to an individual's self-reliance and confidence as well as to his or her capacity to treat others with dignity and compassion.

Encourage a Sense of Community.   The sense of belonging or of interdependence is important in creating an optimal games climate (see Figure 1.6). When youngsters feel connected to and validated by others—that is, when they feel included as an integral part of a game—exciting opportunities unfold. First, when an atmosphere is considered "safe," kids are more willing to take risks—not irresponsible risk, but *dignified daring*. And oftentimes that daring will lead to increased spontaneity, enhanced confidence, or greater determination. And second, a sense of belonging leads to intimate sharing with others and can provoke a shift from shyness and discomfort to openness and the desire to encourage and comfort others.

  As you can see, movement games offer a wealth of possibilities. They carry their own built-in motivation and can be particularly valuable

Figure 1.6 Movement games help children feel included in a group.

for certain children—the reluctant learner for instance, or the child in need of remedial help. The fearful or rebellious, the bored or less-able children often play enthusiastically in a game, which then serves as a powerful incentive for learning and for further participation. Few of us doubt the usefulness of games. What concerns us is suitable games for our purposes. This is the subject of the next two chapters.

CHAPTER 2

HOW TO PLAN AND EVALUATE GAMES

Before learning how to design individual games, it is important to consider the overall games program. A quality games program seldom occurs by whim or by chance. It is usually well-conceived and deserves careful evaluation. Planning and evaluation require time and effort, but they are necessary if you are to effectively accomplish your program goals.

Planning gives direction to a program. Although it is an ongoing process, much planning takes place prior to actually implementing the games; through planning we select goals and design specific games for achieving those goals. We specify expectations and organize the overall program on a long-term basis, and we specify games and modifications to be introduced on a short-term basis.

Evaluation can occur during and after the introduction of a game. We evaluate in order to determine whether our goals have been reached and whether our strategies for implementing the games were effective. We suggest that you approach the use of games in the following manner:

1. Specify your expectations.
2. Plan games experiences consistent with those expectations.
3. Evaluate your program's effectiveness in light of those expectations.

Although this approach is simple to understand and is immediately practical, the process itself is not an easy one—although it becomes easier with experience. The process occurs within a larger framework for presenting games. We will mention the framework briefly, and then return to a discussion of planning and evaluation.

A Model for Presenting Games

Figure 2.1 diagrams a model for developing and presenting games programs. The model, modified from one that we developed in earlier works (Morris & Stiehl, 1985), begins with purposes, which serve as

PURPOSES → PLANNING → IMPLEMENTATION → EVALUATION

Figure 2.1 Designing games programs.

the program's foundation. From that foundation, a program is developed and presented in a logical way, each step based on the preceding one. Evaluation provides feedback for any of the previous steps.

Purposes are formulated from one's beliefs and values concerning such things as the nature of children, the usefulness of games, and the importance of certain types of subject matter. Purposes may be considered expectations you intend to derive from the game. Some purposes discussed in the previous chapter include enhancing skill development, nurturing feelings of self-worth, and fostering enjoyment and satisfaction. Though you may adopt other purposes, you should state clearly those which you regard as fundamental to your program. They will guide the program and be the yardstick against which you can measure the program's success.

Planning first requires that you review your stated purposes and decide which of those purposes you will encourage in a game or series of games. Next, you must design games experiences that will be consistent with your chosen expectations. If the games experiences are inconsistent with the purposes, then the games "package" is suspect. Planning also includes selecting equipment, arranging for use of playing areas, scheduling games sessions, and organizing participants.

Implementation means presenting the games successfully. It includes efficient use of time and resources, conducting the game in a way that is meaningful to the players, encouraging successful performance, recognizing individual differences and using a variety of presentation styles that will benefit each player, and being responsive to the changing needs of players as the game proceeds.

Evaluation is a search for particular kinds of information in light of your purposes or expectations. It may involve observing players' abilities to perform movement skills (see Figure 2.2) or asking them questions about whether they enjoyed the game. It may entail watching social interactions, or testing fitness levels. Perhaps, as in the case of player attitudes, it will require a combination of observations of players and discussions with them. Irrespective of the techniques used, the purpose of evaluation is to gather information about whether your purposes are being achieved. In other words, are you making decisions that will allow you to fulfill your expectations? Are your decisions in the players' best interests? These decisions can relate to the adequacy of your planning, the effectiveness of your implementation, and the appropriateness of the expectations themselves.

Figure 2.2   Players' skills can be evaluated during a game.

Specifying Purposes

Purposes may be formulated at a broad level, covering an entire year's worth of games; at a narrower level, encompassing several weeks or months; or for short-term situations such as a single game. The purpose is to give direction to the games program and to specify what the player will accomplish as a result of the games experience. Here are examples of some skills to be acquired through games in specified lengths of time:

Year: Players will be able to participate in two individual sports and one team sport at an intermediate level of difficulty.

Month: Players will participate in badminton and be able to successfully perform the following: overhand clear, serve, smash, drop, drive, underhand net shots.

Day: In badminton, players will be able to hit a backhand stroke with good form into the opponent's court.

The degree of specificity is determined partially by your level of planning (e.g., year versus single game). It is also determined by your experience and motives. We caution you to avoid stating purposes that are so precise and explicit that the resulting experiences become rigid, narrow, and trivial. We also suggest that your expectations not be so broad that they are impractical either as program guides or as a basis for evaluation.

Planning Games Experiences

Once purposes have been specified, you can begin to organize your games program. The following information is meant to aid you in organizing an overall games program and in selecting a format for describing individual games. The overall plan specifies what players should achieve as a result of the games program. It commonly includes a scope (games or types of games to be offered) and a sequence (order in which they will be offered). When developing an overall plan, it is extremely helpful to organize your games according to some common element.

Some common organizing elements for games are offered, with examples of each:

- Skills: games that involve throwing, catching, kicking, striking, running
- Equipment: net games, racquet games, stick games, beanbag games
- Number of players: 2-player games, 3-player games, small group games, large group games
- Outcomes: cooperative games, competitive games, academic learning games
- Themes: decision-making, socialization, understanding the body in space
- Seasonal sport: football, soccer, basketball, baseball, hockey
- Location: turf and lawn games, street games, court games, water games

Figure 2.3 Many elements can be used to classify games.

- Smorgasbord: relay games, low organization games, target games, net games, invasion games, striking/fielding games

These categories are neither mutually exclusive nor exhaustive. Obviously, there is no commonly accepted strategy for classifying games (see Figure 2.3). The worth of these categories to you is that they enable you to classify your games in a manner that permits rapid retrieval. It is frustrating to vaguely recall a game that you would like to use, and then discover that obtaining it from among hundreds of other games is a bleak prospect. Our intention here has been to suggest some organizing schemes from which you can develop a plan suited to your personal needs and interests. Your scheme constitutes the potential *scope* of your games program.

Once you have decided on an overall scheme, you can identify those games that will be included in a particular program. The games you choose should be the ones that will best assist you in realizing your program purposes. Your selection will also depend on such considerations as availability of time and resources. The games *sequence* for your program is the proposed order in which you plan to present your games. Sequencing may cover a long term or only a single session (when more than one game is used).

In this example the expectations include enhancing the basic skills of passing, catching, guarding, dribbling, and shooting. Table 2.1 gives an example of one games leader's use of scope and sequence.

Table 2.1 Sample Scope and Sequence for Basketball-Type Games

Session	Game	Basic Skills				
		Passing	Catching	Guarding	Dribbling	Shooting
1–3	Guard ball	X	X	X		
	Bull in the ring	X	X	X		
	Circle target	X	X	X		
4–6	Basket baseball	X	X		X	
	9-court basketball	X	X	X		X
	Net basketball	X	X	X	X	
7–12	Dribble contest				X	
	Fast break	X	X	X	X	
	Target ball	X	X	X	X	
13–15	Sideline basketball	X	X	X		X
	Half-court basketball	X	X	X	X	X

First, expectations relative to basketball games were decided upon. In all likelihood, the games leader pondered various questions: What do I want to accomplish? Do I want the players to acquire specific movement skills; or should they be learning game strategies and rules; or will I perhaps concentrate on competing and cooperating? Am I primarily concerned about what happens to each player, or will my emphasis be on the game itself? Many other questions will arise, but the point here is that you should seriously contemplate what you are trying to accomplish during your time with the players. As you begin to lead games sessions, notice how valuable this sort of self-check process can be.

Second, the games leader estimated players' current functioning levels relative to the decided-upon purposes. As discussed later in this chapter, the means for determining "where players are as compared to where you want them eventually to be" will be dictated by the type of expectations you have for them. The information garnered in this type of inquiry will give you a clearer idea of what you can realistically expect to accomplish.

Third, availability of time and resources was examined. For instance, how many total sessions are planned and what is the time allotted to each session? Will all players be at all sessions? What kind and how much equipment is necessary and available? Are there safe and adequate facilities such as a gym, playing field, swimming pool, playground, or multi-purpose room?

Fourth, taking into consideration the aforementioned constraints (i.e., availability of time and resources, interests and abilities of the players), several games were identified as being most useful in light of the stated expectations and were arranged in some suitable order. Even without knowing the nature of any of the games, we might guess that they generally increased in difficulty from the first to the last session. Furthermore, judging from the skills emphasized in each game, it appears that players would have to become somewhat proficient at one skill before proceeding to games that emphasized another. In all likelihood each game or group of games led to the next.

The games listed in the basketball example may have been drawn from a pool of already developed games, or perhaps at least some of them represent modified or novel games created by the games leader. When describing a game, whether traditional or new, it is helpful to use a consistent format. We have found the following format (Figure 2.4) especially useful because it helps focus our attention on important decisions to which we must attend.

Game code _____   Game title _____

Purpose(s): State your general intentions or expected outcomes.

Objects used: Materials/equipment needed for this game; include types, quantity, location.

Organizational pattern: How and where you want players during the session.

Description: Use language that is meaningful to you; describe generally what the game will look like.

Alternatives: Apply procedure for analyzing and designing games. Increase or decrease degree of difficulty (D of D). Using this information, prepare to make adjustments during the game.

Figure 2.4   Game card format for describing a game.

The *Code* serves simply to assist in filing and retrieving the game. For instance, "C-M-22" may indicate that this is number *22* in the list of *court* games that are *moderate* in degree of difficulty. Any code that works for you is the right one. The *Purpose(s)* section lists some suggested purposes and can be useful in cross-referencing the games card. The *Description* section provides a general overview of the activity—its rules, boundaries, method of scoring, and things of that nature. *Objects used* and *Organizational pattern* contain information that will allow us to make decisions prior to engaging the players. The preplanning afforded by these two sections can greatly reduce later confusion concerning players and the equipment needed. Finally, the *Alternatives* section provides variations of the main game. In order to accommodate a wider range of abilities, for example, you may wish to include several easier activities along with several more difficult ones. Or, for motivation's sake, it may be useful to have a few variations that simply add an interesting twist to a game. This can be a great relief when many players are losing interest in a game, yet 10 minutes still remain in a session!

A sample game card patterned after the format described is shown in Figure 2.5.

A few closing thoughts about planning might be worthwhile. When planning games, be willing to begin with only a few goals. Many of

Game code _____   Game title _Four Square_____

Purpose: To enhance striking and reception skills.

Objects used: Playground ball/
              volleyball

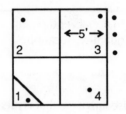

Organizational pattern: • = player

Description: The player in the service square must stay behind the diagonal line when serving. The ball is served by dropping it and serving it underhand from a bounce. If the serve hits the line, the server is out. The server can hit the ball after it has hit once in his or her square. The receiver directs the ball to any other square with an underhand hit. Play continues until one player fails to return the ball or commits a fault. Faults include hitting sidearm or overhand; landing the ball on the line *between* the squares; stepping into another square to play the ball; catching or carrying the ball; touching the ball with other than a hand. The player who misses or commits a fault goes to the end of the waiting line and all players move up. (The player at the head of the waiting line moves into square 4.)

Alternatives: Hitting with the fist, back of the hand, elbow, foot, knee. For example, the server calls out "fisties" to set the pattern.

Server calls out a word; each player must add a letter when returning the ball until the word is completely spelled.

Cannot hit the circle (hoop or rope) placed in the middle of the squares.

Cannot hit the circle (rope) placed in one player's square.

More than one player allowed in a square.

Two-square, three-square.

Groups compete for consecutive successful volleys.

Waiting players can play the ball.

More skilled player(s) must use nonpreferred hand (or be on skates; or use elbows and knees only).

Use more than one ball.

Use a Nerf ball.

Use paddles.

Figure 2.5 Sample game card.

us tend to want to accomplish too much too soon. Then when expectations are not fulfilled, we and our players can all be disappointed. We do not suggest that you settle for less than you and your players are capable of. Rather, we encourage you to set realistic goals. Some teachers include players in establishing goals, which often leads to successful games experiences.

Another suggestion is to prepare yourself for some sessions to advance more slowly than others. Although you may be consistent in your enthusiasm for each game session, some players may not be. For this reason, the daily plan should always be considered a guide rather than a contract to be fulfilled. More positively, you should also be prepared for those days when the players go beyond your expectations—and demand more! Planning for these contingencies emotionally as well as mechanically (i.e., using various equipment, altering playing areas, reducing or increasing time together) can assist greatly in ensuring successful sessions.

In chapter 4 we provide you with substantial information about the next, and most critical, aspect of the games model: *implementation*. As you begin to implement your program, the discussion of assessment and evaluation should prove helpful in determining the effectiveness of your efforts.

Evaluating Program Effectiveness

By conducting valid evaluations, we can gain an accurate, detailed account of a games program's effectiveness. The primary indicator of program effectiveness rests with the players. Are they acquiring the skills, knowledge, and attitudes anticipated in the program plan? A secondary indicator is the program itself. Did the program occur on schedule and in the way it was intended? Were necessary personnel and materials available from the outset? Were the facilities adequate? Were time allotments reasonable? Answers to such questions can be used to identify deficiencies in a program as well as to evaluate success.

We use evaluations essentially to judge and to fine-tune a program. Our evaluations may be fairly superficial or may be quite thorough. When presenting games we frequently engage in *hip-pocket evaluations*— that is, evaluations which must be made quickly without time for careful consideration. Situations often occur in which we must not only diagnose a problem but also prescribe, without time for reflection, a remedy for it. This process is so continuous and routine that it is seldom graced with the name "evaluation."

More formal evaluation requires us to produce valid, precise, and applicable information about the program and the players. Reference has been made already to a few areas of the program that deserve attention (e.g., adequacy of facilities and equipment). Regarding the players, evaluation should be related directly to your stated expectations. You might ask questions like, "Are players progressing toward program purposes? If so, how much progress are they making? To what extent can their success be attributed to the experiences they have had in this games environment?" Naturally, depending on your program goals, certain kinds of information will be more valuable than others. The following examples are meant to illustrate only a few of the many information-gathering possibilities that you can use.

Skill Acquisition. Whether players have acquired movement skills may be determined by using *product* and *process* techniques. Product techniques measure output or outcome such as how fast a player runs, or how far he or she throws a ball. There are many skill tests that are easy to administer and the results are often easily understood. Examples of elements on such tests are the

- number of arrows in the target; the number in the bull's-eye;
- number of baskets in 10 attempts; the number of successive baskets;
- distance the unicycle is ridden straight ahead; the distance ridden among cones;
- time required to dribble the ball through the obstacle course; and
- distance run in 12 minutes.

Improvement in players' product scores over time suggests a program's success.

A process strategy does not concern so much *how far* a player throws as *how* she or he throws; or not *how long* she or he can juggle, but *how* she or he juggles. The focus is on a description of the movement and requires the games leader to develop observation skills for each of the skills to be evaluated. You must know essentially what is required in performing each task and then must be able to judge the quality of a player's performance. The *task complexity spectrum* (see chapter 3) is useful in this regard because it assists in analyzing a skill.

Fitness. Although many fitness tests exist, one preferred test for youngsters is the *Physical Best Test* (1987). A description of the test, along with norms, may be acquired from the American Alliance for Health, Physical Education, Recreation and Dance (AAHPERD). This 4-item test measures aspects of fitness that are related to and predictive of health. The test is designed for children ages 6 to 18.

Test Item	Fitness Component
Sum of triceps and subscapular skinfolds	*Body fatness*
Sit-and-reach (inches)	*Flexibility*
Bent-knee situps	*Abdominal strength*
Mile walk/run (see Figure 2.6)	*Cardiorespiratory endurance*

Figure 2.6 One way of evaluating a games program is by testing the participants' fitness.

Participation.   We assess participation because, in addition to enhancing players' physical and motor proficiency, we also accept responsibility for promoting their enthusiastic involvement in games and physical activity. If participation is stressed at younger ages, children should gain positive feelings about games and about themselves through games.

Participation resists precise definition and, therefore, is not easily measured. For our purposes participation implies active, enthusiastic, physical, emotional, and social involvement in games (see Figure 2.7). We are interested in such questions as the following:

- How long does a player stay fully engaged? In what kinds of games?
- Do players communicate effectively?
- Is a player able to accept criticism and support? To provide it?
- Is the player confident or comfortable when performing in games?

Because no single evaluation strategy has proven totally satisfactory for answering such questions, we continue to adopt methods that provide information most valuable to a particular situation. As you read the following examples, keep in mind that the primary purpose is to evaluate player participation.

Figure 2.7 Participation implies active, enthusiastic involvement.

Hip-pocket evaluation can be an initial and useful means of examining participation. Players' enjoyment of games are noted in the smiles on their faces, the excitement in their voices, the energy in their movements, the enthusiasm of their responses, their lack of inhibitions, and their persistence at the games. In most instances, the differences between players who enjoy games and those who do not are apparent through casual observation. We may, however, desire more complete information.

Several indications that a player enjoys games are the player's positive feelings toward games, as well as his or her persistence and cooperation. Much can be discovered about the latter two qualities by observing them directly; however, positive feelings may better be measured by asking players questions. The following examples illustrate some simple means for evaluating players' interests as well as their feelings about themselves and games.

Sometimes it may be helpful to ask what activities a player likes or dislikes. The following *Activity Interest Scale* (Figure 2.8) allows the player to rate how much he or she enjoys selected activities.

Activity Interest Scale

	Dislike	OK	Enjoy
Soccer	1	2	3
Basketball	1	2	3
Softball	1	2	3
Racing	1	2	3
Volleyball	1	2	3
Archery	1	2	3
Badminton	1	2	3
Bowling	1	2	3

Figure 2.8   Sample interest scale.

The list may, of course, be modified to comprise activities that you wish to make available to your players. Moreover, you can ask players to suggest activities not on the list, to select those they most want to play, or to add comments as they see fit. For very young players and for those who have difficulty reading and writing, you may read aloud each item. The scale can also be simplified by substituting pictures (☹, ☺, ☺) for ratings of 1, 2, and 3. It should be noted that a player's responses must not be regarded as permanent, especially those of younger players for whom interests rapidly change after exposure to new experiences. Nonetheless, this type of scale can offer valuable insight to a player's feelings toward activities and can provide a basis for more in-depth probing, especially with the player who is less than enthusiastic.

A format similar to the one just presented is shown in the *Games Attitude Scale* (Figure 2.9). In this rating scale, the player selects a point between two opposite descriptors that best represents his or her attitude. The scale should be carefully worded, consistent, and allow for clear choices.

Games Attitude Scale

Boring	X	X	X	X	X	Fun
My favorite subject	X	X	X	X	X	A waste of time
Very enjoyable	X	X	X	X	X	Too much work
Something I'd rather watch than do	X	X	X	X	X	Something I'd rather do than watch
Frustrating	X	X	X	X	X	Satisfying
Worthwhile	X	X	X	X	X	Worthless
Dull	X	X	X	X	X	Thrilling
Unhealthy	X	X	X	X	X	Healthy
Feminine	X	X	X	X	X	Masculine

Figure 2.9 Sample attitude scale toward games. *Note.* From *PHYSICAL EDUCATION: FROM INTENT TO ACTION* by G.S. Don Morris and Jim Stiehl, copyright © 1985 Merrill Publishing Company, Columbus, Ohio. Reprinted by permission.

Player Attitude Scale

When I play games, I feel

popular	—	unpopular
weak	—	strong
relaxed	—	tense
attractive	—	unattractive
healthy	—	unhealthy
smooth	—	jerky
accepted	—	unaccepted
rigid	—	flexible
coordinated	—	uncoordinated
most skilled	—	least skilled

Figure 2.10 Sample attitude scale toward one's feelings in games. *Note.* From *PHYSICAL EDUCATION: FROM INTENT TO ACTION* by G.S. Don Morris and Jim Stiehl, copyright © 1985 Merrill Publishing Company, Columbus, Ohio. Reprinted by permission.

The *Player Attitude Scale* shown in Figure 2.10 offers one variation. This scale has a general heading such as "When I play games I feel," and players complete the statement by making their responses to pairs of descriptive terms. In this scale you may wish to substitute other pairs of alternatives (e.g., serious/playful). You might also want to be specific about the games played.

When using these scales we need to ask, "How accurate an indication of feelings is the written response of a player to a question about feelings?" A player's responses are valid only if you can support them with observations of his or her true feelings. Ultimately, you will have to judge whether your players are reliable reporters of their own feelings. The preceding examples are but a few ways of assessing players' attitudes toward activity and toward themselves in activity. We should ask both, "What activities do you like or dislike?" and "How do you feel about yourself in those activities?"

Observing the behaviors of players during games might be the easiest and the most reliable method for assessing participation. Empathy, understanding racial and sex-role stereotyping, willingness to share and to take turns, and acceptance of suggestions and criticism from peers all indicate an ability to participate with others. Evelyn Schurr (1980) suggests that we assess the following social behaviors as a youngster engages in game activities:

- Shares equipment readily
- Takes turns in order
- Makes contributions of ideas in group problem-solving
- Accepts suggestions and criticism from peers
- Accepts decisions of officials and leaders
- Abides by rules, even if no one is watching
- Carries out assigned responsibilities
- Helps others
- Does not exaggerate or cheat in order to be first or to win
- Does not appear tense or anxious when practicing or playing

Another indication of a player's willingness to participate is his or her confidence. Though a relatively new area of study, apparently a youngster's confidence in movement situations may be influenced by

- his or her sense of ability in games (or in a particular game);
- the game's potential physical harm (e.g., falling down) or emotional harm (e.g., being laughed at); and

- the expected sensations (e.g., being upside down) that can result from movement.

Keogh, Griffin, and Spector (1981) identified several observable characteristics of movement confidence. These characteristics can be presented in the form of a checklist as shown in Figure 2.11.

Confidence Checklist

Preparatory movements (occur while getting into position and waiting to move)

_____ appropriate movement to starting position

_____ appropriate waiting position

_____ unnecessary movements

_____ protective movements

Performance movements (occur from initiating movement to completing movement)

_____ task performed in a complete and appropriate manner from start to finish

_____ unnecessary movements

_____ protective movements

_____ incomplete performance

Tempo (hesitations, interruptions, or stops, and excessively fast or slow movements)

_____ movement preparation and movement performance done at an appropriate pace and in a continuous manner

_____ not continuous

_____ too slow or too fast

_____ hesitates, stops, retreats

_____ refuses to perform

Attending (auditory and visual focus, particularly a narrowing of focus through excessive attention to one aspect of the situation)

_____ auditory and visual focus as expected

_____ unnecessary focus on body parts

_____ unnecessary focus on equipment and other aspects of environment

_____ attending excessively to instructor

Figure 2.11 Sample confidence checklist. *Note.* From "Observer Perceptions of Movement Confidence" by J.F. Keogh, N.S. Griffin, and R. Spector, 1981, *Research Quarterly for Exercise and Sport*, **52**, p. 472. Copyright 1981 by the American Alliance for Health, Physical Education, Recreation and Dance. Adapted by permission.

Any useful checklist will need to take into account the observable characteristics that distinguish a player who moves confidently from one who displays a lack of confidence. The signs are often linked to the demands of the game or movement activity. Also, care must be taken to differentiate behaviors associated with movement confidence from those indicating boredom, enthusiasm, or other states. For example, "splashing in the pool may be an indicator of confidence for a young and experienced child, while indicating lack of confidence for an older and more inexperienced child who is avoiding the task demand of swimming across the pool" (Griffin & Keogh, 1981, p. 33).

If a player's level of confidence detracts from participation, we need to assess that level of confidence with accuracy and then attempt to enhance the youngster's confidence by systematically changing games. Naturally, the process of increasing a youngster's participation by elevating his or her level of confidence may not be a simple matter. The concepts of confidence, self-esteem, and sense of self are being studied with revived interest (Bandura, 1977, 1981; Harter, 1983). We know that children, age eight and older, are capable of making judgments about their overall self-worth and that such judgments can influence their performance and participation. Furthermore, much of the self-judging seems to result from youngsters' *perceptions of competence*

Figure 2.12 Games can be used to promote self-esteem.

in domains that they themselves have deemed important, and also by their perceptions of *what important others think of them*.

With regard to self-esteem as related to the physical domain, Weiss and associates (Weiss, 1987; Weiss, Bredemeier, & Shewchuk, 1986) have been investigating the development of children's self-esteem, how self-esteem relates to participation, factors that may influence that relationship, and ways in which positive changes in children's self-esteem can be promoted (see Figure 2.12). In chapter 4 we will discuss the work of Weiss and others as it relates to offering games that will promote self-esteem and evoke the participation of a wide spectrum of players.

In sum, planning and evaluation are integral parts of any quality games program. Planning involves stating purposes or expectations and then organizing games experiences that will aid in achieving desired outcomes. Evaluation involves determining whether those outcomes are reached and whether our strategies for achieving them are effective. In the next chapter we offer a framework for designing games.

CHAPTER 3

HOW TO DESIGN GAMES

In some fashion, games are a part of every child's life. Whether you look indoors or outdoors, in winter or summer, in the city or country, on the seashore, in woodlands, or in the snow, you can usually find children who are playing games; they play in their backyards, on school grounds, in parks, in vacant lots, in gymnasiums, and in streets. The games they play are often derived from many sources from various countries. Some are common, thoroughly tried, traditional games. Others are variations of popular games. Still others are quite novel. Some require standardized equipment; others make use of stones, pebbles, old T-shirts, holes in the sand, and diagrams drawn on the ground. We adults formalize many of these games and offer them to children, usually with some purpose (either stated or implicit) in mind.

In conversations with hundreds of teachers who lead children in games, the most frequent request has been for games that accomplish some expected outcome while, at the same time, accommodating or including all participating children. A difficult request, yes, but our intent in this chapter is to fulfill it. We will demonstrate how *you* can design games that will achieve your purposes as well as include every participant.

Effective games provide congruity between *purposes* or what one intends to accomplish (i.e., expectations such as those listed in the previous chapter) and the nature of the *players* (i.e., their skill levels, interests, and needs). When asking, "What do I intend to accomplish, and what characterizes my players?," the primary consideration is whether a game's structure and demands will allow for *purpose-player congruity*. In other words, we must understand our purposes and our players before creating a game that accommodates both.

Designing appropriate games requires three steps:

1. Understanding the basic structure underlying all games
2. Modifying the basic game structure
3. Managing the resultant game's degree of difficulty

This procedure is adapted from a more detailed one (Morris & Stiehl, 1985) designed to match the nature of *any* participant to *any* movement activity (e.g., dance, gymnastics, swimming, running).

Step One: Understanding Any Game's Basic Structure

When selecting, altering, or creating games in order to satisfy the demand for purpose-player congruity, there are various aspects of games about which decisions must be made. For example, how many players will be involved, and what are their assignments and duties? What is the object of the game? How is it scored? What equipment is necessary? What is the layout of the playing area? Are there officials? Are there rules or restrictions? The list is seemingly endless.

In order to simplify the decision-making process we can begin to cluster some of these different game aspects. We will present only one of many possible ways to cluster the decisions that must be addressed in designing games. There are other possibilities, yet the clusters offered here have been used successfully for more than 15 years. We will refer to the clusters as game *categories*, each of which has additional subdivisions termed game *components*. As depicted in Table 3.1, the categories and their components constitute the bricks and mortar of any game.

As we present the model in greater detail, keep in mind that although the categories and components are useful, you may discover clusters more suitable for your own use.

Purposes.   The first two categories, purposes and players, are critical if we are to insure purpose-player congruity. Purposes can range from very simple (such as "to promote cooperation") to more complex (such as "to improve concentration, to promote thoughtfulness of others, to perform successfully a variety of body-coordination and balance tasks, and to develop strength and cardiovascular endurance"). Furthermore, in a single game you may wish to promote a single purpose, or many. To avoid frustration, however, we suggest not trying to accomplish too many things by way of a single game. It is useful to sequence your purposes and to present them over a defined period of time. We will discuss this process more in the chapter on presenting games.

The eventual game must facilitate some purpose. Purposes from the previous chapter were classified within the following topics:

- Motor skills
- Self-worth
- Fitness
- Enjoyment and satisfaction
- Cognitive skills

Table 3.1 Games Design Model

Purposes	Players	Movements	Objects	Organization	Limits
Develop motor skills	Individuals	Types	Types/uses	Types	Performance
Enhance self-worth	Groups	Location	Quantity	Location	Environment
Improve fitness	Numbers	Quality	Location	Quantity	
Enjoyment		Relationships			
Satisfaction		Quantity			
Develop cognitive skills		Sequence			

Figure 3.1 Games can be used to enhance cognitive skills.

Each of these purposes might be subdivided; for instance, cognitive skills (see Figure 3.1) might be outlined as follows:

- Acquiring knowledge
- Comprehending (interpreting, translating)
- Applying knowledge to a variety of situations
- Analyzing (identifying key relationships)
- Synthesizing (arranging an entire structure)
- Evaluating (making judgments)

These are by no means the only purposes to be used when designing games. Hoffman and associates (1981), who work extensively with elementary-school youngsters in physical education settings, might use the following purposes:

- Becoming aware
- Becoming independent

- Accepting and expressing feelings and ideas
- Accepting responsibilities and acting cooperatively
- Improving quality of response
- Drawing relationships

And Terry Orlick (1978), long involved with the cooperative-games movement, might suggest these purposes:

- Cooperation
- Acceptance
- Involvement
- Fun

We are not promoting one set of purposes over another. Just as we have settled upon purposes that suit our personal beliefs and intentions, you will need to select those that you find suitable. But regardless of your chosen purposes, it is important to establish them clearly. Purposes bring into focus what you are trying to accomplish and prescribe the commitment that you have to your games players. They give direction to you and your players.

Players.   All games have players, but the number of players, their abilities, and other characteristics differ from game to game. Table 3.2 charts some of the decisions that can be made regarding players.

Initially you must decide who will be included in the game, and then to what extent and in what manner. Perhaps only very young children, or only handicapped youngsters, or only highly-skilled players will participate; or perhaps there will be a combination of ages, skill levels, and handicaps together with the nonhandicapped (see Figure 3.2). By attending to *meaningful* player characteristics, you can begin to define the types of games that may be most attractive and relevant to those players. For instance, it may be helpful to know whether a player is skilled or unskilled. It may also be meaningful to know that one child has poor self-esteem, another has a strong need to win, and yet another needs considerable assistance with basic movement skills. It may be further profitable to know whether a child is visually impaired, is gifted, has asthma, enjoys baseball, and so on. An important question is, "Am I attending to meaningful and useful player characteristics?" There is no clear-cut answer to this question. But it is imperative that, in light of the game's purposes, individual player characteristics be considered carefully.

Along with individual player characteristics, you should decide which group characteristics are important. Because most games involve interactions among several players, it is helpful to consider the group's composition and how that may affect the design of a game. Will the group

Table 3.2   Players Component of the Games Design Model

Individual characteristics	Group characteristics	Numbers
Skilled/unskilled	Equal/unequal skills	Individuals
Male/female	Same sex/coed	Groups
Handicapped/nonhandicapped	Heterogeneous/homogeneous	Individuals per group

Figure 3.2 Players' ages, levels of skill, and experience must be considered.

consist of various skill levels? Of children small of stature? Of a wide age range? Of mostly girls? As with individual players, there are numerous dimensions in which a group may be classified. And again, the question is, how useful is that classification scheme?

Some group classifications are more likely than others to influence the nature of a game. You may, for example, group players according to physical size, age, ability, color of eyes, length of hair, first letter of their last name, or color of clothes. Obviously some of these grouping strategies can affect a game substantially; others may have little or no effect.

Last, you will want to make some quantity decisions about players. How many individuals will play? How many at one time? Will there be more than one group? If so, how many? How many players will comprise each group? Will group sizes be equal or unequal? By this point you have likely noticed that decisions about players relate closely to the purpose of the game as well as to such considerations as size of the playing area and availability of equipment.

Decisions about games are seldom made in isolation; rather, one set of decisions always affects another set.

In some cases the decisions will be yours, while at other times the decisions will be made for you.

Movement.   Because all of our games include movement, we place considerable emphasis on its many uses and its variety of forms. We look at the types of movements, where they are to be performed, how much or how many are appropriate, their quality, and so forth. The movements we select will be determined to some degree by our types of purposes (see Figure 3.3, Table 3.3). For example, if our purpose involves fitness, we may include movements that enhance cardio-respiratory functioning, strength, body composition, and other physical attributes. If we are interested in the development of bodily control, then we include body-awareness movements.

Figure 3.3   Movements chosen for a game should suit its purposes.

We might decide where and how the movements will occur. Perhaps they are to occur in one's own area ("location-personal space") while maintaining a crouched position ("location-low level") or perhaps in the larger area ("general space") as the players move in different pathways, traveling in various directions. How quickly or slowly ("quality") should the players move? Should the movements be performed with other players ("relationships"), such as with a partner, or in a small group? Should the movements include use of balls, ropes, or hoops, such as dribbling a ball while running, or jumping a rope while moving backwards? What amount of movement is to be performed ("quantity")? Will the player have three shooting opportunities at the basket? Must each player jump rope for 15 seconds before returning to home plate? In the relay, will all players unicycle for 50 feet, then walk on stilts

Table 3.3 Movement Component of the Games Design Model

Types	Locations	Quality	Relationships	Quantity	Sequences
Physical attributes	Personal space	Force	Objects	Number	Task order within an episode
Locomotor/nonlocomotor	levels	Flow	Players	Unit of time	
Reception/propulsion	directions	Speed	Group	Distance/location	
Body awareness	planes				
	pathways				
	General space				

for 25 feet before returning to their team? As with the other categories, the purpose of the activity—among other conditions—will influence many of your choices.

Objects.   As we design a game, we usually ask what types of equipment or materials will promote the desired purpose. In many traditional games, the equipment itself directs the nature of the game (see Figure 3.4). We also have opportunities to modify existing equipment, to replace it, or perhaps eliminate it altogether *if* such changes allow us to accomplish our purpose and include all players. In Table 3.4 we provide some possibilities for examining the types and uses of equipment, as well as its amount and placement.

One way of organizing materials is to classify objects according to how they may be used. Children can move around, under, over, and through such things as mats, ropes, and hoops. (For instance, they can do cartwheels on mats, or around cones, or from one rope to another.) The can also use certain objects, such as skates and unicycles, to assist them in moving. The two categories ("moving in relation to" and "being moved by") can be combined—as when children use ramps and cones to build an obstacle course through which they navigate on skates, skateboards, or unicycles.

Figure 3.4 Objects included in a game will influence the players' movements.

Table 3.4 Objects Component of the Games Design Model

Types and uses	Quantity	Location
Moving in relation to:	None	Piece-piece
hurdles	One	Piece-player
mats	Several	Piece-group
ropes	Many	
balls		
hoops		
Being moved by:		
skates		
bicycles		
unicycles		
Sending away with:		
bats		
hockey sticks		
feet and hands		
racquets		
Gathering in with:		
gloves		
hands		
lacrosse sticks		
milk cartons		

Some objects are useful for absorbing force and for gathering in or deflecting other objects. Gloves, mitts, certain sticks, racquets, and scoops made from milk cartons are examples. Similarly, some objects can be used to send away or propel other objects; for example, sticks, racquets, and bats for hitting, feet for kicking, and hands for pushing and striking. With imagination, almost any object can serve some purpose. Can you see possibilities for nylon stockings, repaired inner tubes, yarn, milk cartons, oatmeal boxes, deflated playground balls, an old shoe, or a broken baseball bat? We will suggest varied uses for these and other pieces of equipment when we describe games in later chapters.

It is worthwhile to notice that much equipment has multiple uses. A Hula Hoop can be used as a target, as a base, as a "safe zone," or as something to throw, catch, or move through. Racquets can be used to propel objects, to deflect them, or to gather them in. Use a milk carton to receive objects or as the object to be received. There are many ways to determine how an object may be used—game limits, skill ability of the players, and desired outcome, among others.

You may decide to use no equipment at all. You may decide to use only one piece of equipment. If you want to increase each child's on-task time, to reduce waiting time, and to reduce the amount of time spent positioning and arranging equipment, then you must consider the number and types of objects. It is no surprise that some children become frustrated and impatient when they are forced to wait for a piece of equipment or are expected to use equipment that is not geared to their developmental needs and abilities. These considerations will be dealt with again later, because failure to make appropriate decisions in the area of equipment can result in disappointing game experiences.

The final set of decisions involves how pieces of equipment will be located relative to one another and to the players. Prior to its use, should the equipment be near or far from the players? How can equipment be positioned and grouped for easy accessibility before and during play? If a player has limited mobility, can the equipment be placed closer to that individual to provide greater opportunity for success? How can the lack of appropriate choices influence the behavior of the players?

Organization.   Three sets of decisions require attention in this category: the pattern, the number of players in the pattern, and the location of each player (Table 3.5).

The first decisions concern organizational patterns that are numerous and varied. Some games have a fairly well-defined structure with players

Table 3.5   Organization Component of the Games Design Model

Types	Quantity	Location
Defined structure	Even/odd	Players
File	Constant/variable	Group
Circle		Objects
Zone		
Diamond		
Undefined structure		
Random		
Near the fence		

grouped in a line, in a circle, or in a diamond shape. Some have a more loosely-defined structure, such as randomly scattered, or lined along a wall, or "each of you locate your own personal space." A related second decision concerns the number of players in the selected configurations. Will each group have an even or odd number of players? Will the numbers remain consistent throughout the game, or can they change?

A third decision involves the location of players relative to one another, and of groups relative to one another and to the equipment. For example, you may wish to consider the proximity of players as they await turns in a relay game. Some players may need to be far enough away from other players in order to preclude annoying behaviors. Or as they toss and catch a ball, it may be helpful to establish an appropriate distance between players. These location decisions may be more important in some cases than in others. Supposedly, major league baseball would be altered drastically by only slightly altering the distance from home plate to first base.

These are but a few examples of organizational decisions (see Figure 3.5). They will become more obvious as you peruse the games we have selected to present in later chapters. By preplanning organizational decisions and sharing them with your players, you can reduce the number and length of potential management episodes.

Figure 3.5 Another organizational pattern to consider.

Limits.   All games have limits. The nature of the limits is related to what we expect of players and to the conditions imposed by the environment (Table 3.6).

Some movements will be either *acceptable* or *necessary* and others will not. It may be acceptable to run with a ball in football, but not in basketball. It may be acceptable to run to, but not through, the long-jump pit. In some relays it may be necessary to go around every obstacle, while in others it may be necessary to go around only a few.

Table 3.6 Limits Component of the Games Design Model

Players	Environment
Movements	Physical aspects
Acceptable/unacceptable	Geographic boundaries of playing surface
Necessary/unnecessary	Equipment
Participation	Number of players
Acceptable/unacceptable	Activity conditions
Necessary/unnecessary	Time of play
	Scoring
	Rules

In some games, certain forms of participation may be acceptable or necessary, and not so in others. The form of touching that is acceptable, even necessary, in football is neither acceptable nor necessary in basketball. Similarly, in baseball almost an entire team is required to sit down for periods of time; in soccer this would be completely unacceptable. If a game is to be effective, the kinds of movement and participation behaviors that are appropriate or inappropriate to that game should be communicated to each player.

Regarding environmental conditions, the *physical aspects* of the situation as well as the aspects of the game deserve consideration. Physical aspects are observable elements such as boundaries, objects, and the size of teams. Choices here will certainly affect movement time/waiting time ratios. To illustrate, with only four 15-player teams in a relay, the ratio may favor waiting. By allowing more teams with fewer players per team, the ratio shifts in favor of moving. A simple idea, yet not practiced often enough. Is it surprising that some children get bored with some of our games? Why must there be 11 soccer players per team? Can the number be reduced? If not, why not?

It is necessary to make certain decisions about limitations in the activity itself. How long is an inning? (3 outs? 4 outs? 5 minutes? long enough for everyone to have a chance at bat?). How long does the game last? (9 innings? 6 innings? until a set time?). How can one score? (ball in the hoop = 2 points? twice in succession = 4 points plus a bonus point?). What is allowed and what is not allowed? (only two teams on the field? three teams on the field? passing the ball only to players on the field? passing to players on the sidelines?). It may be obvious to you that the limits category can be easily influenced by any of the other categories. Decisions made in one category may call for additional decisions to be made in the limits category. Games designers and games players must understand this particular relationship, as its implications can be important in developing players' self-esteem. The limits category can be especially useful in shifting decisions from the games leader as designer to the games player as designer. Later we will discuss further the option of allowing players to create governing limits.

The intent of this discussion has been to familiarize you with a means for analyzing any game. The categories represent common aspects of all games. By focusing on relevant aspects of a game, you can begin the process of accommodating all players while also achieving the purposes for which the game is used. The next step in designing games requires you to manipulate the aspects of a game in order to change the game or to create a new one.

Step Two: Modifying a Game's Basic Structure

In this step you begin manipulating a game's design. You will expand the components of the model presented in Step One and add specific alternatives to create planned change. Your first task is to select any movement game you are familiar with. Once you have chosen a game, describe it using the model in Table 3.1. Describe the game by asking such questions as: What is the game's purpose? Who will play? How will the players be grouped? How many players in each group? What types of movements are necessary? By continuing this procedure across all categories, you will have separated your game into many elements.

Your next task is to focus on a single category. For many of us it is simplest to begin with the movement category. Imagine (create) some possibilities of movement not already listed in the analysis of your game. As you list each new possibility, try to avoid attaching a value judgment to it. Let your responses come freely. Judgments such as, "No, that would never work," or "That would break the rules," or even "What a great idea!" can impede creativity. The intent here is to create alternatives, not necessarily to discover the best ones. The following example may assist you:

Game: Movement relay
Category to be modified: Movement
Alternatives: 1. Skip backward

2. Run backward, carrying a ball

3. Ride a skateboard

4. Walk on hands only

5. Skip rope down alone, and back with partner

Repeat this exercise using all of the categories and components from Table 3.1. This procedure will take some time, but you will have generated many alternatives.

After completing this task, you might feel ready to proceed to the next one. If not, repeat the task, using another game that you enjoy.

The next task is to select a game with which you are quite familiar. This time make a change, but not an extreme one, in the game's purpose. Again using Table 3.1, examine each game category and decide whether that category might assist you in accomplishing the new purpose. Then, in each of the selected categories, generate alternatives within any components that seem appropriate to you.

We have found it worthwhile to proceed slowly, carefully, and patiently. It is helpful to repeat the previously described exercise with other games. If you practice this strategy rather than rushing ahead, you may find important benefits in terms of your ability to create alternatives. Do not be afraid to test some of your alternatives with willing participants. Again, an example may be useful. The game to be modified is kickball. The change in the game purpose is to decrease waiting time for the offensive team (those that kick the ball). We decided that the organization category and the limits category might assist in our intended change of purpose.

Game: Kickball
Category: Organization
Component: Quantity
Alternatives: 1. Divide the kicking team into 3 subteams.

2. Divide the kicking team into 4 subteams.

3. Divide the kicking team into 5 subteams.

Category: Limits
Component: Players
Alternatives: 1. 3 subteams: one kicks; another performs specified fitness tasks; another rests. Continue at bat until all 3 subteams perform all 3 tasks.

2. 4 subteams: one kicks; another performs balance beam tasks; another shoots baskets; the other rests. Again continue at bat until each subteam has performed each set of tasks.

3. Can you create alternatives based on the last organizational change made above?

Several years ago at UCLA, a women's activity class taught by Dr. Camille Brown became excited with the possibility of modifying basketball in such a way that they could include a variety of skill levels. In order to experiment with their newly discovered talent, they found a group of men involved in a game of pick-up basketball, and promptly challenged them to a contest. Their only stipulation was that the women be allowed to make a predetermined number of modifications in the game beforehand. One of the modifications, for example, was that the men could score points in the usual manner, whereas the women could score 2 points for making a basket and 1 point if the ball hit the rim or backboard. Their rationale was that the men were more skilled, and that this change would encourage the women players to attempt more shots. The men, however, immediately interpreted this change as distorting the game of basketball. Nonetheless, with some reluctance they agreed to accept the challenge.

Much to everyone's surprise, a lively game ensued with both teams enjoying the competition. From this experience, we all learned that initial judgments about game changes can stifle imagination and limit possibilities.

In the example just described, a poor initial judgment almost limited possibilities to the extent that the game—which turned out to be enjoyed by all—could not have been played.

Is it now becoming more apparent how changes in one category can interact with changes in another? Summarizing to this point, we have

- noted that certain sets of decisions common to all games require our attention;
- clustered these sets into several categories, each with subcategories or components;
- asked you to alter some of these components—first for the sake of alteration itself, and then to accomplish some stated purpose; and
- reiterated that game designs should be altered if it will enhance the player's game experience.

At this point you have conducted some game modification using an already established game. With a bit of deliberation, a knowledge that certain sets of decisions (i.e., decisions on players, organization, limits) will influence the nature of a game, and a continued willingness to avoid imposing judgments on the alternatives that you generate, you should also be able to create an entirely new game. But the idea of creating a game on your own might make you feel uncomfortable. Remember—any hesitancy you might have probably stems less from inability than from an unwillingness to create something novel. The fear (or reluctance) to create is not overcome by talent, nor genius, nor instruction—but by persistence.

Step Three: Managing a Game's Degree of Difficulty

Although this step could be considered a substep of Step Two, we choose to treat it separately because it deals directly with the continuum of skills, abilities, and needs that exists among games players. By modifying a game's degree of difficulty (D of D), we can provide experiences that challenge and satisfy all players.

Once again, we find it easiest to work in the movement category first. The difficulty of a movement task can be increased or decreased by examining and then altering its complexity. To do this, you must first recognize that all motor skills are rather complex—that is, they have many components. For instance, a tennis serve has the following components: stance, grip, ball toss, backswing, forward swing, ball contact, and follow-through. Altering any one of these components can affect performance.

Besides the movement itself, there are other factors that can either limit or facilitate a person's performance. Among these factors are the size of the playing area, the size and type of racquet to be used, the weight and diameter of the ball, and the height of the net. In modifying D of D, we can manipulate such things as the number of task components to be performed, the size of a ball, the length of a lever, the amount of support available for performing on a unicycle, the speed of an object, the size and distance of a target, and so on.

We have found it helpful to approach D of D through a sequence of three action steps.

Action 1: Identify the Factors That May Limit a Player's Performance.   In the example involving a tennis serve, some factors mentioned were the player's stance and swing and external factors such as size of the ball and height of the net. The only factors to list here are those that can be modified by you or the player. So, although a player's visual perception, for example, may be an important factor, unless we can influence it directly we should not list it as a factor that can be modified.

Action 2: Diagram the Task Complexity Spectrum.   Any task can be made more or less challenging. The task complexity (TC) spectrum is a continuum of task descriptors that are sequentially arranged from less difficult to more difficult. For instance, a TC spectrum for the factor "ball size" as it affects a player's ability to strike a moving ball might look like this:

TC	Ball size
Easy	Large
↓	Medium
Difficult	Small

The idea is that striking a large ball is less difficult than striking a smaller one. Even without an extensive background in analyzing movement tasks, you can, with practice, begin to diagram how a task might be made more or less challenging to a player.

Action 3: Begin to Create Tasks That Vary in Difficulty.   Continuing with our example of striking a ball, we have already considered size of the ball as a factor to be manipulated (see Figure 3.6). Another factor is whether the ball is moving. A stationary ball is easier to hit than a moving ball; a slow-moving ball is easier to hit than a fast-moving ball; and a fast, straight-moving ball is easier to hit than one with

Figure 3.6   Three tasks that vary in difficulty.

considerable spin. Now, combining size of ball with movement of ball, we can create some easy to difficult tasks:

TC	Task
Easy	Strike a large ball off a batting tee.
	Strike a medium size ball off a batting tee.
	Strike a small ball off a batting tee.
	Strike a slow-moving large ball.
	Strike a faster-moving large ball.
Difficult	Strike a slow-moving small ball.

Determine what constitutes *large, medium* and *small* by evaluating your players' entry skill levels (i.e., the ability each displays when you plan to introduce the game). Also, when you consider factors in combination (e.g., size of ball *and* whether it is moving), you must determine the relative importance of each factor. For instance, is it more difficult to strike a large, moving ball or a small, stationary one? If you wish to pursue a more in-depth examination of task-difficulty and task-complexity, we recommend Richard Magill's *Motor Learning: Concepts and Applications* (1985).

In the appendix we offer a few examples of the TC spectrum as applied to several movement skills (i.e., kicking, catching, jumping, throwing, and striking). Our intent is to show you how the TC spectrum can be used to modify various aspects of games. By modifying aspects of games, a wide range of player abilities can be accommodated.

In each game category there are many many possible alternatives. By modifying them, we can design games that vary in complexity (see Table 3.7).

Table 3.7   Modifying Degree of Difficulty Using Limits and Players

Category	Modification
Limits	
Physical aspects	Can you increase/decrease the size of the playing area?
	Can you use different types of equipment?
	Can teams have different numbers of players?
Activity conditions	Can you have a turn-limit game?
	Can a basket be worth five points?
	Could you add up total points of both teams, and if they equal a predetermined score, a winner is declared?
Players	
Characteristics	Could players of different ages and sizes play together?
Quantity	What happens if one team has more players than another?
	In soccer, could there be more than two teams on the field at the same time?

In review, the process of changing games involves essentially three stages: understanding the basic structure of games in general, modifying that structure for a specific game, and altering the game's degree of difficulty. We'll now share a strategy for utilizing this process.

A Strategy for Designing Games

Assuming that you have some sense of what you want to accomplish with your players (i.e., purposes or expectations), you'll want to collect some pertinent information relative to the players' current functioning levels. Again, the type of information collected will be determined by your purposes. If, for example, your interest is in skill development, you may wish to observe players' movements and record their performance in some fashion. Many possibilities exist for gathering different types of information; some involve formal assessment while others are much less formal. The idea is to collect *useful* information.

Once we know what the players can do, it is necessary to determine which variables will likely influence their performance. In the games model, the *equipment* and *movement* categories are often useful in this regard. We have already mentioned some of the variables that can influence, for example, a player's locomotor and reception skills. To

Table 3.8 Propulsion Skills—Factors Influencing Kicking and Striking

	Ball size	Ball color/ background color	Ball shape	Ball movement	Angle of trajectory	Reception location
Easy	Large	Yellow/black	Round	Stationary	Horizontal	Body midline
	Medium	Blue/white	Oblong	Rolling slowly on ground	Vertical	Preferred side
Difficult	Small	Yellow/white	Irregular	Rolling rapidly on ground	Arc	Nonpreferred side

further illustrate, in Table 3.8 we identify some factors that might influence the performance of such propulsion skills as kicking or striking.

Interpretation of this figure suggests that kicking a relatively large ball is easier than kicking a small ball. As games leaders, we can offer players an opportunity to identify their own level of challenge by allowing them to select from a wide variety of, say, batting implements, objects to be batted, speeds and angles of the projectiles, and so on.

To keep records of player performance, you might consider creating a profile as demonstrated in Table 3.9. Here we illustrate one player's striking performance as related to size of object and color of object.

Profile sheets can be designed to include any suspected performance factors. Although multiple factors can be examined, we recommend beginning with only one. As you become more comfortable with the use of profile sheets, combinations can be considered. Many combinations are possible, and we include several examples based on physical attributes and locomotive patterns in the appendix.

Depending on your goals, you may decide to use some of the suggestions just presented in order to make a game more challenging or less challenging. Children in sandlots, in backyards, and on playgrounds

Table 3.9   Propulsion Skills—Kicking and Striking Profile

		Easy ⟶ Difficult		
		S_1	S_2	S_3
Easy	C_1	Success 2/4/87	Success 2/4/87	Tried but failed 2/8/87
↓	C_2	Success 2/5/87	Success 2/5/87	
Difficult	C_3	Success 2/5/87	Tried but failed 2/8/87	

Key: Object size (S)
S_1 = 12″ rubber ball
S_2 = 8″ rubber ball
S_3 = 6″ rubber ball

Key: Object color (C)
C_1 = blue
C_2 = yellow
C_3 = white

Player's name _____

have been modifying games haphazardly for years. However, by using the steps outlined in this chapter, you can design games in a manner that will allow you to achieve planned outcomes. The next chapter explores some strategies for presenting games in an effective manner.

CHAPTER 4

HOW TO PRESENT GAMES

A bad games leader is like a magician who believes the magic lies in the magic kit rather than in the minds of the audience. As a result, something is usually missing. Perhaps the stage is not set properly, a consequence of an error in *planning*. Perhaps the sleight of hand is too slow, and at a crucial moment the audience is allowed to see where the rabbit really comes from. The audience groans, and the magician's ineptitude is embarrassingly apparent. The magician has made an error in *presentation*.

Presenting a game is not merely a matter of setting out the props or of "kicking open the doors and throwing out the balls." No games, no matter how good, are teacher-proof. A good game will appear to run itself; but behind that appearance is the care, energy, and time of a games director. If you take the pains to present games effectively, set the stage right, eliminate awkward moves, and direct the players' attention to the hat and away from yourself, your players just might experience magic of a kind—the magic of moving, perceiving, learning, and engaging in things they have never experienced before.

In this chapter we deal with the implementation component of the games model presented in chapter 2. We are not going to discuss numerous teaching styles or teaching methods, identifying the situations in which each style may be used advantageously. We will suggest, however, some tips for presenting games. Each set of tips or suggestions is in response to questions most often directed toward us as we teach games. Generally speaking, becoming a good games director takes preparation and practice—preparation that involves selecting and designing games that will achieve your purposes, and practice at offering the games in a manner that invites the enthusiastic participation of each player.

How Do I Prepare Myself to Present Games?

For some, one of the most difficult lessons to learn about presenting games is to stay flexible. When you direct a game, you assume the role of facilitator or guide. While the children are playing a game, you should watch, listen, encourage, and help as needed. Those of you who regularly run interactive activities, and who are used to the noise and apparent disorder that come with them, will have no trouble creating the relaxed, productive atmosphere in which games flourish. On the other hand, if you like to remain at a distance from children, and if you value order and formality in group settings, then you may need to adjust to the noise levels and physical activity that movement games require. Suppress your qualms, relax, and try a game just once. Chances are good that the game will work out to your satisfaction, especially if you are willing to persist and are open to other suggestions that follow.

Assume that you have somehow acquired a game that seems suitable to your purposes. Your first job is to get to know that game intimately—its purposes, its mechanics, its rules, its organization, and its demands for space, equipment, and time. In doing so, you will likely begin to generate ideas for tailoring the game to fit the interests and talents of your players. Perhaps you will find others who have played similar games and who can tell you how players have responded to it, what they learned from it, what "bumpy spots" to expect, and what modifications might be useful.

However you go about acquainting yourself with the game, keep asking yourself whether it will accomplish what you intend it to. Further, keep a mental list of the assumptions the game may make about the players. By knowing how well your players can meet the demands of the game in its present form, you will be better prepared to make modifications if necessary. Also keep in mind the opposite possibility: are your players already so proficient at the game's demands that playing the game would be superfluous?

Whether the players will view a game as boring, enjoyable, or somewhere in between depends largely on the games climate: that is, leader-player and player-player relations in your games setting. Obviously you cannot alter established relationships with a single game; but to the extent that you can influence the mood of the group, you should try to create an atmosphere of serious fun. Keep the introduction brief; try not to launch into a long drill session on rules or on practicing skills necessary for participating in the game. Rules are boring and confusing to read or hear; they are best learned through actual play. On the other hand, if you decide that certain unfamiliar elements deserve players' time, then devise games and activities to teach these elements before introducing the game.

Once the game has begun, remain as unobtrusive as possible. Your main job now is to observe and listen. Try not to interfere. Play may move slowly at first, but momentum will build as players grow more comfortable with the rules and other expectations. Also, try not to change the game too frequently, especially in its early stages. Players usually want to become comfortable with the basics before trying alternatives.

During the initial stages of confusion, players will ask questions. Always avoid as much elaboration as you can, yet answer the question completely, and fast. If disputes between players arise, encourage them to work out solutions themselves. Sometimes a situation will require guidance from you. For example, it is almost inevitable that one player will accuse another of cheating. In such instances you may decide to briefly stop the game and ask the accuser (in this case, Lori) to explain the broken rule to the accused (Kerry). Then ask Kerry if she understands the rule. If so, continue the game; if not, assist Lori with her explanation. If Kerry breaks the rule again, say, "Kerry, you said you understood the rule. Do you? Show me." A third infraction might require you to offer a contingency—something like, "Kerry, you understand the rule, but you've broken it again. Now you have a choice. You may continue to play if you abide by the rule, but if you break the rule you must sit out for a while." If Kerry breaks the rule again, you should make her sit out, but be sure it is clear to Kerry that the choice was hers: "Kerry, I see that *you* have decided to sit out for a while." This way, you are not seen as the "bad guy."

Sometimes players challenge the rules and propose modifications. (This is usually a healthy development—we will discuss it in the section on enhancing creativity.) Briefly, help the players think through the consequences of their change in terms of the whole game. If they are willing to accept those consequences, let them. Be reluctant to restrict their ideas; when you must arbitrate, be consistent with the goals and with the spirit of the game.

How Do I Enhance Creative Problem-Solving Through Games?

A problem begins with a perceived difficulty. It can be argued that youngsters have neither the store of information nor the command of their creative talents necessary to solve a problem with a creative solution. However, research on problem-solving in children indicates that they likely go through processes that parallel the creative processes of adults. Furthermore, we might expect that the circumstances most conducive to the development and encouragement of creative talent in adults would be those most conducive to parallel processes in children.

The greatest handicap to creative problem-solving in adults is fixedness of thinking—an inflexibility of assumptions or beliefs that stifles fresh ideas. Adults are also handicapped by fears of failure and of being wrong. Preschool children, on the other hand, typically fail in problem-solving for different reasons: They fail to understand the problem, they forget the elements of the problem, or they lack sufficient information. The school-age youngster shares the handicaps of the pre-schooler, but, with a growing sensitivity to social judgments, he or she is also handicapped by fear of failure. A youngster may be so distressed at the prospect of being wrong that the question or problem is not even heard or the task not even attempted.

We recall one of our early teaching experiences. One particular high school P.E. class displayed a full spectrum of abilities and interests. In addition to those sincerely interested in physical activity, we taught bullies, social isolates, physically awkward, and perennially uninterested students, as well as a few athletes who "didn't need to take physical education." One day, as had happened on numerous previous occasions, many of the students drifted unenthusiastically in to class . . . late. So, we felt, the day had arrived to step out on the edge and take a risk.

Other classes were using much of the available equipment, so we made a pile of "leftovers" that included: two bats (one of which was broken in half); eight bases; and five balls of varying sizes, shapes, and inflation. We then posed the following challenge to the class: Create a softball game that uses all of this equipment and involves every single player in the class. We engaged the class in games analysis, and, within a short time, the students had created the most outrageous game the school had ever seen. To this day we do not understand all the aspects of the game—yet each player did!

They met our challenge; everyone was accommodated. Batters could choose the type and size of ball to be hit, the manner in which the ball would be delivered, and to which base they would initially run. What appeared to us to be confused base-running was actually, to the players, a well-orchestrated traffic pattern. Other aspects of the game included: three teams competing against one another simultaneously, the defensive team able to score points, and players rotating onto and off all three teams (thereby never knowing which was their home team).

For the remainder of the school year the spirit and enthusiasm of that class overwhelmed us. Many of the players began to create their own homework assignments, which they housed in their newly constructed "P.E. notebooks." We discovered that by teaching the class games analysis strategies, and by granting permission to employ the strategies, the ownership of the games (as well as responsibility for receiving value from a physical education program) shifted from us to them.

How might creative problem-solving be facilitated? To begin, we offer several principles (adapted from Torrance, 1965) that you might follow in encouraging your players:

- Be respectful of unusual questions.
- Be respectful of imaginative, creative ideas.
- Show players that their ideas have value.
- Occasionally have players do something for practice without any threat of evaluation.

Creative individuals tend to be described as impulsive, sensitive, self-confident, independent, and unconventional. If you wish to foster creativity, you must be prepared to encourage a wide variety of behaviors and ideas. A setting of clear boundary conditions is important, but so is tolerance of independence, autonomy, the unconventional, and the nonconforming.

In games, it is important that players engage in generating alternatives. Players create new games by producing alternatives to existing games; they solve problems by producing alternative solutions. One approach we have found successful in providing creative games experiences (and this has worked with players from age 6 to 76) is as follows:

Step 1.   Introduce the notion that any game can be played with several possible alternatives. Select a game that is familiar to the players, but not one that they have already decided is *the game and not to be changed.* Suggest a few movement alternatives. Play the "new" game(s).

Step 2.   Using appropriate materials (overhead projector, chalkboard, handouts, flip-chart) and the games design model (Figure 2.1), explain how any game can be analyzed and separated into various components (adapt your explanation to the group's level of understanding). Submit the "new" game(s) to analysis using the model.

Step 3.   Select another game. Divide the larger group into small, manageable groups. Permit players to generate alternatives; usually players are most comfortable at offering *movement* alternatives, and then *object* alternatives. In this step it is important to accept *all* alternatives. We find it helpful to list the alternatives on a chalkboard or panel. Sometimes it is also helpful to have the movement category and its components on the chalkboard and to direct the players' attention to some of the descriptors you have listed (or ask players to list their own descriptors).

Step 4.   Select some of the alternatives and try them out with the players (see Figure 4.1). Make adjustments as necessary.

Figure 4.1 Generating alternatives to existing games helps stimulate creativity.

Step 5.   Expand the list to include all categories. Permit the players to continue designing and trying out their new ideas. You must be willing to accept this part of the process as an unfolding. You are giving players permission to think, to play a game differently. It takes time; more thinking and planning than moving may prevail. Set time limits and move among the small groups, offering direction, if necessary or if requested.

Step 6.   Consolidate small groups into a large one. Provide players with a summary of what they have accomplished. Consider sharing the language of activity design with them (i.e., TC spectrum, D of D). They now have an operational framework for creating games.

Step 7.   Use the model and strategy with different games. Do not only modify existing games, but create entirely new ones. You may be surprised at how adept (and enthusiastic) your players will become at creating games.

You can now present problems to players and they will be able to apply games design strategies. For example, here are some player solutions to the question of how to introduce cooperation in a competitive game:

• Instead of an "out" game, use a time-limit game where each team has a designated amount of time on offense and defense.

- Allow players to choose how to score from a number of different scoring methods.
- Develop a system that adds everyone's scores together.

Additional problems might include the following:

- how to include a player with spastic cerebral palsy
- how to increase the amount of playing time for everyone
- how to use the same equipment for different purposes
- how to use several balls of different sizes, colors, and textures to design a net game that requires all players to keep the balls traveling in the air over the net
- in kickball, how to redesign the movements of the defensive team so that more than two players (pitcher & catcher) are continuously and actively involved.
- given a box of hoops and balls, how to design a target game in which the target's distance, height, and size are manipulated in order to accommodate everyone in the group
- one player from each group going to the problem box (a cardboard box filled with game categories with pertinent descriptors written on pieces of paper), selecting a piece of paper, returning to the group, and within 10 minutes designing a game using only the components listed on the paper
- taking into consideration the abilities of everyone in a group, how to design a striking game that permits everyone to be involved at the same time, with each player choosing how the object is to be delivered and which striking implement will be used

Problems like these may be presented by you, or they may occur in the natural course of game playing—when players interact with other moving players; when target locations change; when the location or type of equipment shifts; when another team's strengths and weaknesses call for a change of strategy. All of these situations require players to engage in convergent and divergent thought. Problems assist players in realizing why rules are necessary, how a change in one category may require decisions in another, how there can be a place for everyone's abilities, and how a game's design relates to game strategies.

Besides seeking solutions to game problems, players may also define the problems. Cultivating the ability to independently discover and design new problems is at the heart of games design. At the very least, the opportunity to modify games will increase possibilities for success. Incorrect responses seldom exist as all alternatives contribute, in some way, to addressing the problem at hand. We have also found that discipline becomes a minor consideration when players' physical as well as mental abilities are being challenged.

The most critical aspect of the creative problem-solving process is to not reveal—by look, word, or deed—what you think of a player's alternatives (within the constraints of safety, of course). A player's sense of success, or lack of it, should come from within the game, not from the intrusion of the games leader, no matter how perceptive and unbiased the leader may be. For the same reason, we suggest that you not judge players' performance while they are trying out game alternatives. It is essential that they be willing to risk mistakes. This willingness is unlikely in an atmosphere of evaluation.

Here are a few final suggestions:

- Allow players to make errors.
- Allow players to use their own solutions even if you know of better ones.
- Permit players to proceed at their own pace.
- Expect a certain amount of noise and disorder.
- Be prepared to admit a lack of knowledge about an aspect of the game being studied.

How Do I Enhance Self-Esteem Through Games?

Many games leaders view self-esteem or self-concept development as an important part of their program. Self-esteem can be defined as one's personal judgments and feelings of worthiness. Self-esteem is important in game settings because it can influence a player's motivation, persistence, standards of success, and the reasons given by the player for success and failure. Variables that can affect a player's sense of worthiness include the player's

- level of *competence* (both actual and perceived) in meeting achievement demands;
- *social acceptance* by important others (such as parents, teachers, coaches, and peers); and
- *control*, or feelings of personal responsibility for successes and failures.

In order to enhance self-esteem, it is not enough simply to build success experiences into games. Self-esteem development requires a variety of strategies. Many of the games strategies that follow are drawn from our own experiences with youngsters and from the work of Weiss and her colleagues (1986; 1987).

1. *Using appropriate feedback and reinforcement.* Your evaluations of a player's performance should be accurate and fair. Although

some games leaders tend to give high amounts of reinforcement, it has been found that excessive praise of mediocre performances or for success at simple tasks can convey low expectations to a player, possibly lowering that player's confidence. At the same time, too much criticism can give a player the message that higher levels of achievement are expected. Simply stated, encouragement should be honest; that is, it should be contingent on successful performance or for striving toward a realistic goal.

2. *Helping players understand why they succeed or fail.* Players should understand why their performances are successful or unsuccessful. The degree of this understanding is powerfully related to their perceived competence. For players who take personal responsibility for success, their resultant positive attitude leads to future participation. This does not hold true for the player who attributes success to external factors, such as luck or task ease. Conversely, if players take personal responsibility for lack of success (e.g., did not practice enough, did not try very hard), they will likely realize that they can change future outcomes. If lack of success is dealt with appropriately (e.g., attribution-retraining, as discussed by Dweck & Elliott, 1984), then failures can be experienced responsibly by the players with reduced impact on their developing self-esteem. For instance, a failure attributed to lack of practice is likely to be perceived as less negative than one attributed to lack of ability, as the player can realize that similar failures in the future are not necessarily inevitable. As you notice players' successes and failures, assist the players in attributing successes to ability or skill and unsuccessful attempts to lack of practice.

3. *Focusing on optimal challenges.* As we have discussed elsewhere (Morris & Stiehl, 1985), the demands of the game should match the capabilities of the players. A game that offers optimal challenges will motivate players to engage in the activity and to persist at it. Players derive great enjoyment and satisfaction from mastering skills optimal to their potential (see Figure 4.2). Players who succeed at a task *below* their optimum may say the task was too easy; players who succeed *above* their optimum may say they were just lucky—both of which result in no boost in self-esteem. Using the TC spectrum and the D of D concept, you can present games in a way that offers a range of skill difficulties—a range from which players can select their own "optimal" challenges. Similarly, players can design their own games and tasks, thereby having the opportunity to control their own environment.

Figure 4.2 Mastering optimal challenges can be enjoyable and satisfying.

4. *Emphasizing process goals versus outcome goals.* Whereas the primary focus of outcome goals is on the outcome of one's performance (e.g., winning, scoring points), the focus of process goals is to improve one's own performance and increase one's competence. A critical aspect of process goals is that they are under the control of the player. The players set goals and then assign success and lack of success to factors they can control. Players who emphasize outcomes tend to be occupied with gaining favorable (and avoiding unfavorable) judgments from others. Thus, process-oriented players are interested in learning, while the outcome-oriented players can be distracted from personal growth by their emphasis on winning and looking good.

5. *Using indirect styles of teaching.* Offering games to youngsters requires a chain of decision making (e.g., *what* each player must do; *where* the players will be relative to one another and to pieces of equipment; *how* certain types of equipment will be used; and *when* various aspects of the game will begin and end). Your decision about what decisions to share with players can have a profound impact on the game climate which, in turn, can influence player participation. Allow the players to engage in decision making and to use problem-solving methods of inquiry. This style, suggested in the previous section on creative problem-solving, allows players more control over their environment. By giving players some control over the game and involving them

in the game's design, there is greater likelihood for the occurrence of optimal challenges. Another result is that in problem-solving situations, players will likely react to errors as natural and useful, not as an indication of failure. Notice the difference between the player who says, "I have failed three times," and one who says, "I am a failure." An excellent guide for learning how to shift decisions from the games leader to the players is Mosston and Ashworth's work (1986) on a spectrum of teaching styles. You may wish to consider alternative styles of presenting games other than the traditional direct and controlling style with which many of us are familiar.

What Else Can I Do to Assist Players in Changing Games?

As more games designers have experimented with changing games, the following aids have been suggested.

Game Blocks.   Using boxes similar to those available at most gift stores, select a category and write descriptors on each of the box's six sides. Reinforcing the edges with tape prolongs the life of the box (Figure 4.4). Use the games design model (Table 3.1) to assist you in developing descriptors. Game descriptors are provided in Table 4.1.

You can see that descriptors can be centered around specific game components within each category. Players use the blocks as dice as they make decisions about the design of the game. Roll a die; the descriptor facing up becomes part of the game. This is a fun, non-threatening way to introduce games design. Allow players to roll several dice at one time. Certain combinations work well (e.g., movement types with movement quantity; objects types or objects quantity with location). To avoid creating dozens of boxes, consider constructing boxes with replaceable side panels.

By sliding descriptors into the side holders you can constantly change information on the blocks.

Figure 4.4 Game blocks.

Name_____   Date_____

To the student: Read the tasks below carefully.
When ready, begin task 1. Move to the next
task when you have successfully completed
each task.

Tasks	Completed	Needs more time
1. Within the game of volleyball, change two of the movement descriptors. Play a 4 minute game.		
2. Change the ball size and /or height of the net. Play for 4 minutes.		
3. Change one of the limit descriptors to make this a cooperative game.		

Figure 4.3 Task panel.

Task Panels.   The *task panel* is made from poster board and covered with a clear surface designed for use with erasable marker pens (Figure 4.3). You can change each of the descriptors within a category as the sessions progress from one day to the next.

This same information can be copied onto 8½ × 11 task sheets and distributed to players or small groups. It is possible to design the sheets to meet individual player characteristics.

Table 4.1 Game Descriptors

Movement	Objects	Limits
Locomotor	Balls	Most points wins
Run	Hoops	Turn-limit game
Jump	Mats	Time-limit game
Hop	Ropes	All players touch ball
Skip	Bats	Multiple pieces of equipment
Cartwheel	Milk cartons	"Out" game
Reception	Unicycles	Uneven numbers per team
Catch	Gloves	
Gather in		

Game Spinners. The basic concept of game spinners is similar to that of blocks (Figure 4.5). Using concentric rings (made of poster board) affix a moveable arrow in the center of all the rings. Each ring represents descriptors from one game category. Spin the arrow; the designated set of descriptors become those used in the new game (or those changed in the existing game).

Figure 4.5 Game spinners.

Again, you can construct multiple concentric rings and simply interchange them as sessions progress. It is also possible to use material that permits you (or players) to constantly change descriptors. By rotating the position of each ring you offer new combinations of descriptors to the games designers.

Game Surprise Box.   The *game surprise box* works well with younger children (Figure 4.6). Using small cardboard boxes, allow each player to decorate a box with stickers, sports and games heroes, rock groups, and so on. Inside the box, place games design problems (or descriptors) on pieces of paper. In this manner you exert some direction and planned change over the game, yet the players will control the game's final outcome.

Figure 4.6   Game surprise box.

Audiovisual Aids.   These are a few modalities that others have found helpful. You can use overhead transparencies to accomplish the same ends (e.g., draw a game spinner onto a transparency). We have also had success using brief audio-cassette recordings of game tasks. Place cassette tape players at different locations in the movement area. This works well with children as young as six years. We hope these ideas will prompt you and your players to generate many of your own.

How Can I Modify Games Effectively?

The concept of modifying games in order to accomplish specific purposes continues to generate questions among those using these procedures. Some of the as yet unanswered (if they indeed are answerable) questions that teachers, recreation specialists, and youth sports leaders have posed include the following:

- Can we use some of these ideas so that daily practices are conducted more efficiently?
- Can "lead-up" games be more appropriately designed?

- How can we use these concepts to increase practice time and reduce waiting time?
- Do children's soccer fields and other playing areas need to duplicate adult playing areas (e.g., size, boundaries, and shape of field or court; size and location of goals, baskets, etc.)? The same question pertains to children's equipment.
- Would leaders of youth sports programs consider changing established and accepted sports in order to include more children (perhaps by matching the activity to the participants' developmental status, thereby enticing more of them to participate)?
- Should the primary limitation to any game be the creativity and enthusiasm of its participants?

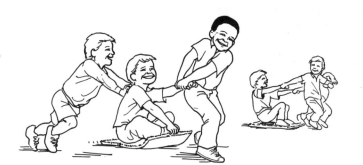

GAME IDEAS

Anyone can change a game, even create one. By this point in the book we hope that you are convinced that games are not sacrosanct. In fact, an avid games maker sees in any existing game dozens of possibilities for new games. During the past 15 years we have witnessed hundreds of children and adults devise literally thousands of games. In this section we will present some of the more familiar game forms as well as a few novel ones. All of the games in this section are workable in that participants have enjoyed playing them in either their present format or with appropriate modifications. To meet the needs, abilities, and interests of your players, you may need to make adjustments in these activities; sometimes these adjustments will be minimal, other times dramatic. If you do choose to make changes, you may wish to consult some of the procedures that we outlined in Part I.

The games included here have been played and designed by people in the United States and in Scandinavia. Not only will each game be described in a consistent manner by using the game card format described in chapter 2, but we will make numerous references as to how the games can be modified using the activity design procedures (ADP) discussed in the preceding chapters. In fact, for every game an *alternatives* format is used so that each game easily begets additional games.

Moreover, in order to prompt you to alter the difficulty of each game and to include all players, we will be asking specific questions concerning possible game modifications. We intend that you conclude this section of the book with at least six variations for each game we present. With your continued input, your "game bank" will increase.

CHAPTER 5

BASIC MOVEMENT GAMES

Basic movement games are designed to provide a foundation that will assist players in reaching their full potential as skillful games players. These games are simple in design, may require pieces of equipment, and incorporate fundamental movements such as running, hopping, skipping, jumping, carrying, throwing, and catching.

By using deliberate teaching strategies and by gradually increasing the difficulty and complexity of the game, these activities introduce the novice games player to movement game experiences. Although these games are frequently used with younger children, they can be played by individuals of all ages and abilities. They are useful, for instance, when introducing players to large-group experiences that may involve cooperation and competition or rules and sanctions. They are also useful for acquainting players with the concept of altering a game's structure.

In terms of movement per se, emphasis is placed on what players' bodies are doing, where they are moving, how they are performing, and the relationships that are occurring as their bodies move. The framework for this aspect of basic movement games is as follows:

- Space utilization: moving in personal and general space in a variety of directions, across different pathways, while performing at different levels
- Relationship interaction: moving in relation to others, to equipment, and to changing spatial requirements
- Quality actions: moving at various speeds with varying degrees of force
- Body understanding: performing general body movements such as locomotor and manipulative actions

For ease of presentation these games have been placed into the following categories: tag, relay, and reception and propulsion. As a game's design changes, the game might be more appropriately classified in one category than another. Perhaps even some different categories evolve.

TAG GAMES

Foot Tag or Pair Tag

Description:

The object of this game is for each player to tag his or her partner's foot using one of his or her own feet. Pairs face one another and join hands. Play begins and ends on a signal from the games leader. Stress to the players that hands must always be held, and partner's feet should be tapped, not stomped.

Objects used:

None

Organizational pattern:

Pairs randomly scattered

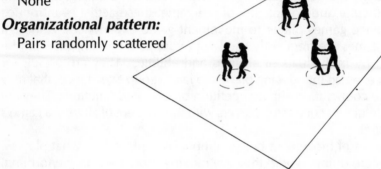

Alternatives:

1. Use a trio of players all holding hands.
2. Define a confined area out of which the pairs may not move.
3. See how many tags are made in 15 seconds, 20 seconds.

What if the pairs held only one hand?

Could you also have players balance some object (e.g., bean bag, sock) on a shoulder or other body part as they attempt to tag their partners?

What would happen if you added up all of the foot tags made in a specified time period and challenged another class to have even fewer tags?

Contributed by: Ellen Haehre—Norway

Same Place Tag

Description:

Each pair has one Nerf ball between them. The player with the ball is "it," and upon the games leader's signal runs after the partner and tags the partner with the ball. The ball is then given to the partner, who becomes the new "it." The object now is for "it" to run after the partner and tag him or her on the same part of the body that "it" was previously tagged.

Objects used:

Nerf balls

Organizational pattern:

Pairs randomly scattered

Alternatives:

1. Play in threes, so that the player with the ball has two players to chase.

2. Change the movement from running to skipping, hopping, or other movement.

3. Change the level of movement (e.g., travel on all fours).

What if players had to carry a large soft ball in one hand and a small tagging ball in the other (without dropping the large ball)?

Could you play this game with pairs of taggers chasing pairs of taggees?

What would happen if the person tagged got to determine the manner in which players now moved?

Contributed by: Ellen Haehre—Norway

Add-On Tag

Description:

The object of this game is for players to be the last tagged. Upon a signal from the games leader, three "its" chase the other players. When tagged, a player joins hands with the "it" who tagged him or her, and both chase the rest of the players. When tagged, players continue to "add on" to the three growing lines. Everyone in the lines is now also "it." After the last player is tagged, the game begins again with three new "its."

Objects used:

None

Organizational pattern:

Three "its" facing randomly scattered group of players

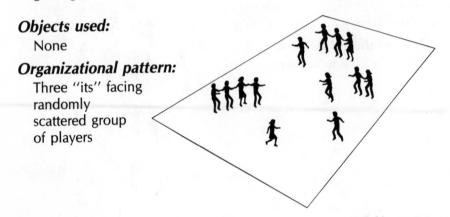

Alternatives:

1. Have fewer or more starting "its."

2. Allow only a confined geographic movement area.

3. As players add on, alternate the direction each faces, such as front, back, front, back.

What if you permitted only certain locomotor movements?

Could you have an area that was considered "safe," where players could not be tagged?

What would happen if after creating a line of four players they divided into pairs and each pair became new "its" and chased after the remaining players?

Catch Me if You Can

Description:
The object is for players never to be tagged with the ball. The teacher or games leader begins play by throwing a ball into the air. A player catches the ball and all players freeze where they are. The player with the ball throws it at someone, and if hit, he or she goes to a predetermined "out" area (e.g., a hoop). If the player catches the ball, the thrower is "out." Play resumes with the games leader again throwing the ball in the air, and the next "out" player takes the previous one's place. The previous "out" player returns to play—thus only one player at a time is out.

Objects used:
Soft rubber ball

Organizational pattern:
Players randomly scattered about a defined area

Alternatives:
1. Use more than one ball.
2. Use different types of balls.
3. Designate the type of throw permitted.

What if you allowed the ball to bounce before it was caught?

Could you allow the ball to be passed to three different players before being thrown?

What would happen if you had teams?

Contributed by: Inge Morisbak—Norway

Snipe-Snorp

Description:

The object of this game is for players to chase and tag the players lying opposite them when the chase command is given by the games leader. One group of players lying in a row is known as "Snipe," the other is "Snorp." When the leader calls "Snipe," all the Snipe players are "its," and the Snorp players get to their feet as quickly as they can and run to their safe area. The Snipe players also jump up and chase the Snorps. If players are tagged before making it to the safe area, they become Snipes and the players who tagged them become Snorps. When the games leader calls "Snorp," then the procedure reverses.

Objects used:

None

Organizational pattern:

Two lines of players lying head-to-head on their backs

Alternatives:

1. Increase the distance of the safe areas from the start position.
2. Place cardboard boxes that must be jumped over on the way to the safe areas.
3. Increase the space between the two groups of players.

What if you gave only a visual cue to begin the game?

Could you have the players start in a back-to-back sitting position?

What would happen if players could tag more than one person at a time?

Contributed by: Halldor Skard—Oslo, Norway

Octopus Tag

Description:

The object is for players to try to make it across the ocean (playing area) to the safe side without being tagged. Each time the games leader signals, players run across the playing area and the two octopi ("its") chase the fish (other players). If a fish is tagged, he or she is frozen in that spot. The immobile fish can tag the running fish, freezing them also. The game is over when almost everyone is caught.

Objects used:

None

Organizational pattern:

Two "its" standing in the middle of the playing area facing the group of players

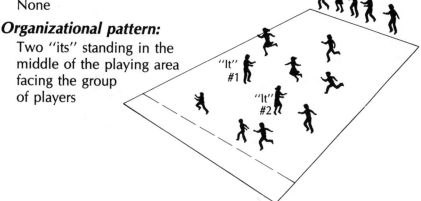

Alternatives:

1. Increase the number of "its."

2. Change the dimensions of the playing area.

3. Permit the frozen players to pivot on one foot, thus giving them greater range of movement.

What if you played this using a three-legged construct (e.g., standing side by side, partners tie their inside legs to one another)?

Could you use balls to tag the players?

What would happen if you gave the octopi only a certain amount of time to catch everyone?

RELAY GAMES

Tractor Race

Description:

On a go signal by the games leader, each of several teams performs side rolls in unison to a predetermined location. The first team across the marker wins. The games leader can also divide each team into two halves (Groups A and B). Group A rolls a designated distance until it reaches Group B. When Group A arrives, Group B begins rolling toward the location from which Group A came. The first team to complete the exchange wins.

Objects used:

None

Organizational pattern:

Teams of players lying side by side

Alternatives:

1. One player at a time rolls to the finish line and back.
2. Players on a team roll as pairs to the finish line and back.
3. Players must hold an object in their hands as they roll (e.g., a paper ball on top of a frisbee).

What if players had to roll up and down a hill made of mats?

Could you have players roll underneath a precariously balanced object without knocking it over?

What would happen if you had everyone on the team balance, collectively, a long object, as the whole group rolled toward the finish line?

Contributed by: Halldor Skard—Oslo, Norway

Take It Back

Description:

The object of this relay is for players to get as many objects as they can from the center area back to their team. On the start signal, one player at a time from each team runs out to the objects, picks one up, and returns. After tagging the returning player's hand, the next player leaves. Play continues until all objects are gone. The team with the most objects is the winner.

Objects used:

Various balls, towels tied into knots, jump ropes, hoops, cones

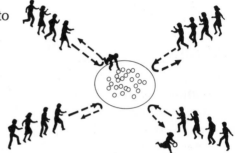

Organizational pattern:

Four-corner relay pattern, each team facing diagonally another team

Alternatives:

1. Change the locomotor movements.

2. Return the objects using only the feet.

3. Change the direction and level of movement (e.g., backward at a low height).

What if players had to weave in and out of teammates upon returning with an object before getting at the end of the line?

Could you require players to move around the entire group before tagging the next player?

What would happen if the game were not over until all of the equipment was put away, one piece at a time?

From Here to There

Description:

The object of this relay race is for players to move their partner, who is sitting on a carpet square, from one location to another as quickly as possible. On a signal from the games leader, movers race to their partner. They move the carpet rider by having each partner hold one hand and pull the carpet rider across the floor. Or one partner can pull, while the other pushes. The first team to return across the movers' start line wins.

Objects used:

Carpet squares

Organizational pattern:

Groups of three—two of three players start at a line 50-100 feet away from the third players

Alternatives:

1. Have more players per group; shuttle players back and forth.
2. Allow other body parts to be pulled (e.g., feet).
3. Increase the distance to be pulled.

What if you changed the body positions to be used on the carpet? Are some positions less safe than others?

Could you have the player being pulled also have to dribble a ball?

What would happen if you placed objects in the way for players to navigate over and around?

Contributed by: Halldor Skard—Oslo, Norway

Keep It Together

Description:

The object of this race is for each pair in a team to complete the following task as quickly as possible. Partners place a knotted towel between their heads, and on the start signal move as a pair down and around a cone and back. Players should not use hands to hold the towel in place. If the towel drops, players may put it back in place and continue. The first team whose pairs complete the race wins.

Objects used:

One towel tied into a knot per pair, playground cones

Organizational pattern:

Teams in a pair column pattern

Alternatives:

1. Change the location of the knotted towel (e.g., between the hips, lower back, legs).

2. Change the organizational pattern to a shuttle, circle, or four-corners formation.

3. See how many times players can complete a trip in two minutes, the team with the most trips wins.

What if players first practiced moving the towel without racing?

Could you make this a throw and catch race?

What would happen if each player had a towel connected to his or her partner's towel, and raced down and back?

Put It in the Mailbox

Description:

The object of this race is to be the first team to complete the following. On the start signal, the first player on each team carries a bean bag to the stall bars. The player climbs up to the top of the bars and drops the bean bag into the "mailbox." The player then climbs back down the bars, retrieves the "mail" (bag), and carries it to the next person in line. Play continues until all players have completed these tasks.

Objects used:

Bean bags, stall bars

Organizational pattern:

Column pattern facing stall bars

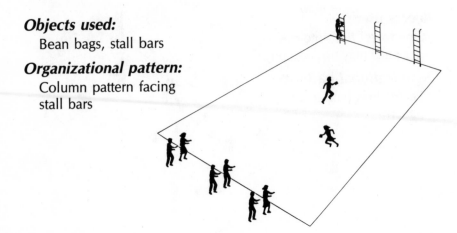

Alternatives:

1. Use more than one bean bag.

2. Increase the distance to stall bars.

3. Change the mode of locomotion (e.g., hop, skip, jump, roll).

What if the game became a turn-limit game or a time-limit game?

Could you see how many "pieces of mail" teams could deliver in two minutes?

What would happen if you put a cardboard box on top of the bars and the players had to put the bean bags into it?

Contributed by: Inge Morisbak—Norway

Hold On

Description:

Teams try to be the first to complete the following tasks. One player hangs from the stall bars with legs in an L-position (knees bent). On the start signal, the first player in each group runs to his or her teammate (hanging from the bars) and places the bean bag on the teammate's knees. Upon being tagged by the returning teammate, the next player repeats the task. Continue until all bean bags are successfully held by the hanging teammate.

Objects used:

Bean bags, stall bars

Organizational pattern:

Column pattern facing stall bars

Alternatives:

1. Change the mode of locomotion.
2. Use other equipment (e.g., balls, ropes, knotted towels).
3. Vary the hanging position (e.g., hold legs in V-position).

Create your own ideas!

What if . . .

Could you . . .

What would happen if . . .

Contributed by: Inge Morisbak—Norway

Snake Along

Description:

The object of this race is for Group A to exchange places with Group B in the following manner. Players on each team in Group A, while lying on their backs on a towel, move across the floor, pushing themselves with their feet and legs. Upon reaching teammates in Group B, each player tags a teammate, who then repeats the same movement back across to Group A. Play continues until everyone has exchanged places.

Objects used:

One towel per player

Organizational pattern:

Shuttle relay pattern

Alternatives:

1. Have players lie on their abdomens and move across the floor.

2. Use a circle pattern, assign a number to each player, who moves around the circle, returning to the starting place. Repeat many times.

3. Change the distance between groups.

What if players had to travel all the way around the opposite group before tagging the next player?

Could you use a four-corners formation and have players sit in a line (on towels) like a train, wrap their legs around the person in front, and move in unison toward the center of floor?

What would happen if the lead player in the preceding game had to carry a medicine ball?

Contributed by: Reidar Hagen—Norway

RECEPTION AND PROPULSION GAMES

Busy Bee

Description:

The object of this game is for the player in the circle to keep the bean bags out of the circle. Upon a start signal, the player with all of the bean bags inside the circle starts throwing them out of the circle. All of the other inside players try to catch the bags thrown in the air and immediately return them to the circle. Play continues for a designated period of time.

Objects used:

Bean bags, ropes

Organizational pattern:

One person standing inside a circle made by ropes, the rest of the players randomly scattered about the area

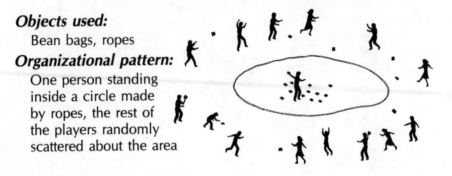

Alternatives:

1. Change the objects used—different sizes, textures, colors.

2. Stop the objects using body parts other than the hands (e.g., feet only).

3. Designate a specific propulsion skill to be used.

What if you increased the size of the circle and had two players inside it?

Could you have multiple circles in a defined geographic area?

What would happen if you had the players move at different levels?

Contributed by: Inge Morisbak—Norway

Keep Your Field Clean

Description:

The object of this game is for teams to keep their side of the benches free of bean bags. The game begins with equal numbers of bean bags on either side of upside down benches. On a start signal, players on both sides propel the bags to the other side of the benches. Play for one minute and stop. Count the bean bags on each side—the team with the fewest number wins.

Objects used:

Bean bags, wooden benches

Organizational pattern:

Two teams—players
randomly scattered
on either side of
benches that are
turned upside down

Alternatives:

1. Use larger bean bags, Nerf balls, paper balls, rubber balls.

2. Use a slanted net, rope, or boxes rather than benches.

3. Permit only certain locomotor movements retrieving objects.

> **What if** you played this game at different levels (e.g., high to low)?
>
> **Could you** use only the lower half of the body in this game?
>
> **What would happen if** you played for a longer period of time and awarded points to different types of equipment?

Contributed by: Inge Morisbak—Norway

10-Pass

Description:

The object of this game is for team members to throw and catch the ball 10 times without the other team intercepting the passes. One point is awarded to the team that catches 10 passes. The ball is then given to the other team to try to accomplish the same task. As the ball is passed among team members, the opposing team is permitted to intercept or deflect the ball. Body contact is not permitted. If a ball is dropped, simply continue play—do not count passes from zero unless one is intercepted by the opposing team.

Objects used:

One playground ball

Organizational pattern:

Two teams of five to ten players randomly placed within a defined geographic area

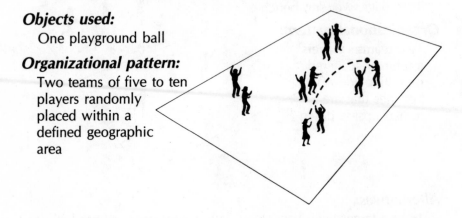

Alternatives:

1. Have a three-second rule (i.e., players are allowed to hold the ball for only three seconds and must then pass the ball).

2. Permit players to take only five steps before they must pass the ball.

3. Change the number of required passes.

> **What if** you allowed more than one ball in the game?
>
> **Could you** put a protective circle around a player in a wheelchair?
>
> **What would happen if** an able-bodied player had to play in a wheelchair? Could you have the wheelchair player count two passes for every one caught?

Contributed by: Inge Morisbak—Norway

The Boxer

Description:

This game requires that players be able to keep a box moving in the air, using different body parts to keep it elevated (e.g., hand-hand, foot-foot, hand-foot, elbow-hand). Upon a start signal, each player sees how long he or she can keep the box in the air, and how many times in a row the box can be hit before it touches the ground.

Objects used:

One small cardboard box per player

Organizational pattern:

Players randomly scattered

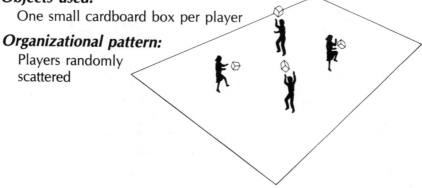

Alternatives:

1. See how many different body parts can be used to keep the box up in the air.
2. Use different size boxes.
3. Keep two boxes moving at the same time.

What if you made this a partner game?

Could you play this game with empty plastic milk cartons?

What would happen if the game was played with three or more in a group who tried to keep their box in the air longer than other groups?

Contributed by: Halldor Skard—Oslo, Norway

Have a Seat

Description:

The object of this game is for players in a large circle to sit on each others' laps at the same time. At a predetermined signal, all players sit down on the knees and thighs of the players immediately behind them. It is important for them to move slowly.

Objects used:

None

Organizational pattern:

One large circle

Note:

This is not a reception and propulsion game. I have used it as an initial "getting to know you" game that precedes many of the basic movement games. To foster a sense of caring for others, players can gently rub another's back, shoulders, and arms. Sensitivity to others is a lesson that can be further enhanced by discussing personal needs and space rights.

CHAPTER 6

BALL GAMES

All games in this chapter include the use of some type of ball. In general, the games are designed for large teams with one team either competing against or cooperating with at least one other team. These games incorporate many of the movement skills discussed previously; however, the games are more complex than the ones in the previous chapter, and they usually involve offensive and defensive strategies. Nonetheless, most of the games can be played by both secondary and elementary school students. By adjusting the degree of difficulty, each game can be matched to the particular players' abilities.

Several of the games originated in Scandinavia, but most of them are familiar to people in America. They can be used for introducing players to various cognitive as well as movement skills. We have grouped the games as follows: invasion games, softball and baseball games, and basketball games. Invasion games require at least two teams, each one defending an area, an object, or another player. Using additional objects or players, each team's territory is "invaded."

INVASION GAMES

Hit the Club

Description:

The object of this game is for teams to try to knock over as many of their opposing team's clubs as possible within a specified time period (up to five minutes per block of time). Neither team is permitted to cross the center dividing line. The balls are to be thrown or rolled at the opposing team's clubs. Players are permitted to use any body part to try to stop the balls before they hit their own clubs. The team knocking over the most clubs at the end of play is declared the winner.

Objects used:

Indian clubs or cartons, medium size
playground balls

Organizational pattern:

Gymnasium divided into
two halves with
teams randomly
scattered in their
own halves

Alternatives:

1. Increase/decrease the number of players on each team.

2. Increase/decrease the number of balls used in the game.

3. Use milk cartons instead of Indian clubs, or mix the two, and award different numbers of points to each.

What if you used Nerf balls?

Could you alter the body position/level of the players (e.g., sitting , kneeling, standing)?

What would happen if you varied the propulsion skills (e.g., kicking, striking)?

Contributed by: Reidar Hagen—Norway

Bombs Away

Description:

The object of this game is for teams to hit the goal ball over the opponent's goal line by throwing or rolling playground balls at the goal ball. One point is awarded each time this occurs. Players are not allowed to use their hands or other body parts to stop or propel the goal ball. Play for a specified time. After a point has been scored, restart the attack by placing the goal ball in the center of the floor. Players must remain behind their goal lines when they throw their balls toward the goal ball.

Objects used:

Wooden benches, playground balls of different sizes

Organizational patterns:

Gymnasium divided into two halves, with teams behind their own goal lines

Alternatives:

1. Increase the number of goal balls.
2. Increase the number of playground balls.
3. Use a different weight goal ball (e.g., a medicine ball).

What if you varied the position/level of all the players (e.g., sitting, kneeling)?

Could you place a volleyball net along the center line and require that all balls go underneath it?

What would happen if you allowed players to use scooters and allowed movement up to the center line?

Contributed by: Reidar Hagen—Norway

Stop Me if You Can

Description:

The object of this game is for teams to get as many of the balls as possible on their opponents' side of the net. The net is raised high enough off the floor so that all the balls can roll underneath it. Players are either sitting or kneeling on the floor. The balls *must* go under the net; use any body part to stop and propel the ball. After four minutes, count the number of balls on each side of the net.

Objects used:

Equal number of playground balls per team and one low net

Organizational pattern:

Gymnasium divided into two halves, each team on either side of the center line

Alternatives:

1. Increase the number of balls
2. Change the type of balls used in the game.
3. Permit players to stand and allow pivoting on only one foot.

What if players had to propel the balls through other players' legs?

Could you permit only certain parts of the body to stop the ball?

What would happen if after one minute the side with the most balls got two players from the other side to join their team?

Contributed by: Reidar Hagen—Norway

On Target

Description:

The object of this game is for teams to score points by rolling a ball past the opposing team, under the center net, rope, or board, so that the ball hits the back wall. The players try to stop the balls using any body part or another ball. Players must always remain in a sitting position, even when chasing after a ball. The area between the two teams and under the divider is called the neutral zone—no one can enter it. Balls in the neutral zone can be moved only by hitting them with other balls, or being handled by the games leader. Play for five minutes.

Objects used:

Four playground balls, a low net, rope, or a board balanced on boxes across the middle of the gymnasium at a low height

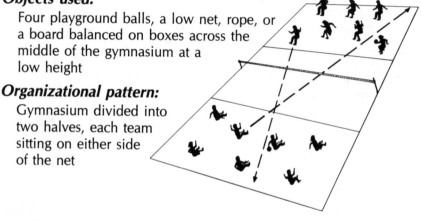

Organizational pattern:

Gymnasium divided into two halves, each team sitting on either side of the net

Alternatives:

1. Add more balls; or try balls of different shapes and textures.
2. Award a team a point if an opposing team player leaves the sitting position.
3. Change the size of the neutral zone.

> **What if** you adjusted the height of the net?
>
> **Could you** add milk cartons to the game (if knocked over three points are awarded)?
>
> **What would happen if** you varied the position of players, added other targets, or made this a cooperative game?

Contributed by: Reidar Hagen—Norway

Go-Bots on the Loose

Description:

The object of this game is for players to remain standing and moving about the area as long as possible. Two players are selected to be "Go-Bots;" each is given two Nerf balls. On a start signal, the Go-Bots invade the other players by throwing the balls at them—if hit, a player must sit down. The way to return to the game is to secure a thrown ball and throw it at another moving player. If the moving player is hit, the sitting player can return to moving about the area, and the hit player must sit down. Thus, a player is never eliminated from the game, and there is a constant change in standing and sitting players. Remember, players are frozen in place when sitting—they can retrieve a ball by stretching to get it.

Objects used:

Eight to ten Nerf balls, playground-ball size

Organizational pattern:

Players randomly scattered about an area

Alternatives:

1. Increase the number of Go-Bots.

2. Use only underhand throws.

3. Have a "safe" area where players cannot be hit with balls.

> **What if** you only allowed the ball to be thrown at players below their waist?
>
> **Could you** play this game in pairs?
>
> **What would happen if** you allowed players to hit the Go-Bots and then exchange places?

SOFTBALL AND BASEBALL GAMES

Three Flies Up

Description:

The object of this game is to catch three fly balls. One player is the kicker and the other two are receivers. The first player to catch three fly balls trades places with the kicker and the count begins again. The ball must be caught in the air for it to be a legal catch.

Objects used:

Playground or soccer balls

Organizational pattern:

One ball per group of three

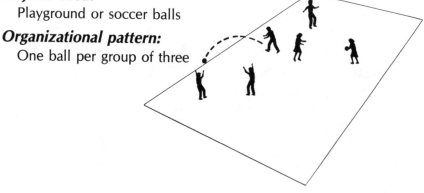

Alternatives:

1. Increase the distance between the kicker and the receivers.
2. Allow the ball to bounce before it is caught.
3. Players must catch the ball three times in a row to become the kicker.

What if you permitted players to kick the ball with only the nondominant foot?

Could you make this a four-, five-, or six-flies-up game?

What would happen if you had players kick the ball over a net or rope?

Contributed by: Philip J. Pinto—age 7

One Base

Description:

This game is similar to traditional softball and baseball except there is only one base. One player at a time goes to bat and remains the batter until he or she hits a pitched ball. The batter then runs to the base, and either stays or returns, depending upon the situation. To score a run, the batter must return to home plate and touch it. The fielding team includes a pitcher, catcher, and other players scattered about the field. Outs are made as in traditional softball and baseball. After two outs or when five runs are scored, the teams trade places.

Objects used:

One ball, one base, a bat

Organizational pattern:

Two teams alternate batting and fielding as in traditional softball and baseball

Alternatives:

1. Vary the distance between the base and home plate.

2. Allow more than one batter to stay on the base.

3. Allow batters to use several different size bats/balls, plus a batting tee. Allow players to decide how the ball is to be delivered.

What if players are declared out if the bat is thrown outside of set boundaries?

Could you make this a one-out game?

What would happen if you had several different base–home plate distances in order to accommodate players who move at different speeds?

Maple Hill Ball

Description:

The object of this game is for players to score as many runs as possible. The batting team is up for only two minutes.

Batters: Hit the ball off the tee, and run to the bowling area. Stay behind the line (12 feet from the pins) and bowl a ball until all pins are knocked over. The batter must retrieve the ball if needed to knock over all the pins. Then run to the home hoop.

Fielders: After the batter hits the ball, one player retrieves it. The rest of the players stand inside their hoops. The ball is then thrown among eight different players. The player receiving the eighth throw runs to the exchange hoop and exchanges the batted ball with another one. The new ball is moved to the out hoop—it must stay *in* the hoop. If all of this occurs before the batter steps inside the home hoop, the batter is out! If the batter steps in the home hoop first, a run is scored.

Objects used:

One batting tee, three bowling pins, hoops, different types of balls

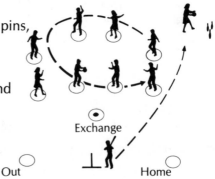

Organizational pattern:

Two teams—alternate batting and fielding positions; game hoops arranged between batter and fielders; bowling area

Alternatives:

1. Increase the distance between the exchange and out hoops.
2. Increase the number of bowling pins; increase the distance between the pins and the bowling line.
3. Permit other striking skills (e.g., hit the ball with a tennis racquet or kick a rolled playground ball).

> ***What if*** you allowed more players to participate?
>
> ***Could you*** make this a turn-limit game (e.g., only three players are at bat at a time)?
>
> ***What would happen if*** you designed tasks other than bowling for the batters to perform?

Figure-Eight Ball

Description:

The object of this game is for teams to score the most runs. It is played similarly to traditional baseball with these adjustments: four outs per inning; three-inning games; the batter remains at bat until the ball is hit; a thrown bat is an automatic out; each batter chooses the type of bat, ball, and delivery; bases are run first through seventh in a figure-eight order (note that batters touch third base twice); and a caught fly, a forced out, or a tag are ways in which a batter is out.

Objects used:

Seven bases (hoops), several types of bats and balls

Organizational pattern:

Two teams—alternate fielding and batting, bases arranged in a figure-eight pattern

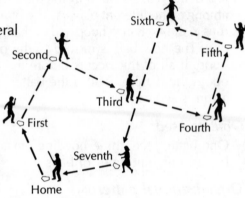

Alternatives:

1. Increase/decrease the number of bases.
2. Play a turn- or time-limit game.
3. Vary the striking movements allowed (e.g., horizontal, underhand, overhead patterns).

What if you permitted players to run the bases in any order?

Could you permit more than one player on a base at a time?

What would happen if you played with only five to seven players per team and had several games in play at the same time?

Maple Hill—Hit and Go

Description:

The object of this game is for teams to score as many runs as possible.

Batters: Divide team members into three groups. Each group gets to have one batting turn per inning (alternate the player who bats). The batter strikes the ball and, together with the rest of the players in the group, runs to the jump rope stretched out on the floor (placed 50-100 feet away in right field). The group members must jump over the rope 10 times and then all return to the home hoop as fast as possible.

Fielders: Begin outside of the hoops and one player fields the batted ball. The rest of the fielders stand inside their hoops. The ball is thrown among eight different players, and the last player to receive a throw runs to the exchange hoop and exchanges the batted ball with another one. That player then moves to the lummi stick and milk cartons. As quickly as possible, he or she balances the lummi stick on top of two upright milk cartons. Then he or she runs to the out hoop, and places the ball inside it. If batters return to the home hoop before the fielders complete their tasks, then one run scores. This is a turn-limit game (each group gets one turn at bat per inning).

Objects used:

One batting tee, hoops, different types of balls, lummi sticks, milk cartons, one jump rope

Organizational pattern:

Two teams—alternate fielding and batting; game hoops arranged between batters and fielders; jump rope and lummi stick areas

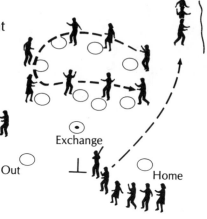

Exchange

Out

Home

Alternatives:

1. Have the fielding team line up in a column; the person retrieving the ball must crawl under the other fielders.

2. Have six to eight bases in a semicircle that batters must run around.

3. Vary the size, shape, and color of the balls.

What if the fielders also had to perform other tasks, such as dribbling a ball, performing rolls, or bowling, while batters also performed other tasks?

Could you allow the fielders to take runs away from the batters by picking up three extra balls from the exchange hoop? Subtract from the batters' score the number of extra balls successfully placed in the hoop.

What would happen if each batting group were allowed to choose one of several tasks (e.g., jumping the rope 10 times, dribbling a ball with feet, kicking toward a target)? The tasks might be arranged in order of difficulty, with harder tasks worth more points.

BASKETBALL GAMES

One on One

Description:

The object of this game is for players to score the most points in four minutes or score a predetermined amount of points as quickly as possible. Hang a Hula Hoop over the basketball rim—award one point if the ball goes through the hoop, and three points if the ball goes through the basketball rim. One player inbounds the ball. The player who scores maintains possession of the ball. Play is similar to traditional basketball.

Objects used:

One basketball per pair, one Hula Hoop

Organizational pattern:

Pairs randomly scattered about a basketball hoop and backboard—several pairs can play per half court

Alternatives:

1. Change the type of ball.
2. Adjust the height of the basket and hoop.
3. Play two on two, three on three, two on one, or three on two.

What if you gradually added certain rules (e.g., traveling, double dribble, no fouling)?

Could you adjust the points awarded for making a basket?

What would happen if you made this a cooperative game?

Pass and Shoot

Description:

Partners face each other, five to seven feet apart. The games leader writes a large P (for pass) and a large S (for shoot) on a blackboard and a number next to each. Players must then pass the ball the amount of times the number indicates. One player moves to a basket and stays there until he or she shoots and scores the number of baskets written under S. Then the player returns the ball to the partner. The first pair to finish wins the game.

Objects used:

One ball per pair

Organizational pattern:

Pairs randomly scattered about the basketball court

Alternatives:

1. Vary the number of passes (no more than 20).
2. Vary the number of shots (no more than five).
3. Change the mode of locomotion to and from the basket.

What if you changed the type of pass used (e.g., bounce pass)?

Could you designate a specific kind of shot to be taken?

What would happen if players had to remain at the basket until they made three out of five shots?

Four Corner Relay

Description:

The first person from each team dribbles to the center of the gym; all four players crisscross with one another. Each player continues diagonally to the opposite corner of the gym, hands the ball off to the next player, and goes to the end of the line. The player who receives the ball dribbles diagonally across the gym. The first team to return all players to their original positions wins the game.

Objects used:

One ball per team

Organizational pattern:

Four-corner relay pattern

Alternatives:

1. Allow carrying the ball.
2. Change the height of dribble allowed.
3. Set up cones that players must travel around.

What if you asked the players to use their nondominant hand?

Could you use this game to teach specific dribbling skills and/or rules?

What would happen if you added a second ball to each team?

Pass and Turn

Description:

The first player from each team dribbles the ball to the opposite end of the gym, then returns, while dribbling, to a spot indicated on the floor. He or she performs a chest-pass to the next teammate in line who, in turn, dribbles to the opposite end of the gym and returns to a mark on the floor (five feet from the first player). He or she then passes the ball to the first player in the line, who turns and passes to the next player in line. This new player, and every other person in line, must weave in and out of the players standing on the gym floor, return to a spot on the floor about five feet from the previous player, pass to the next player, who then turns and passes to the next. Continue in this manner until the ball reaches the starting position. Play continues until each player has participated. The first team to return the ball to the starting position wins the game.

Objects used:

One ball per team

Organizational pattern:

Teams in file pattern facing the other end of gym

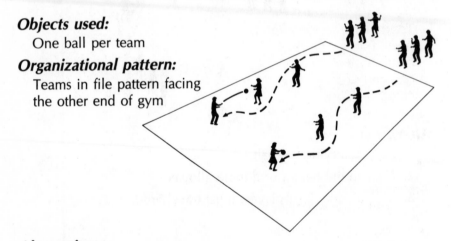

Alternatives:

1. Change dribbling direction.

2. Use only nondominant hand.

3. Dribble two balls.

What if you had to dribble under your teammates?

Could you see how fast each team completed the tasks, add the scores, and compete (time) against the next class?

What would happen if after performing these tasks everyone had one opportunity to shoot a basket?

Basketbowl

Description:

The object of this game is for teams to score as many points as possible. Teams are in any relay pattern. The first player on each team attempts to bowl the ball and knock over a milk carton. After this (only one attempt per person), the player retrieves the ball and moves to the shooting area, where he or she takes one shot at the basket or the Hula Hoop hanging from the basket. The player then gets the rebound and moves back to his or her team and hands the ball to the next player. The team with the most points wins; two points are scored for a basket; one for a hoop; and one for hitting a carton. Play for six minutes.

Objects used:

Variety of balls, Hula Hoops, milk cartons

Organizational pattern:

Teams arranged in a relay pattern on a basketball court; milk cartons on one end of the court, balls for shooting baskets on the other

Alternatives:

1. Add more milk cartons.
2. Increase/decrease the distance between the cartons to the bowling line.
3. Change the point values.

What if you gradually introduced specific basketball rules?

Could you permit players to develop strategies for retrieving the ball?

What would happen if you added a second ball to each group?

Back-to-Back
Basketball

Description:

The object of this game is for teams to score as many points as they can during a specific time period. The only difference between this game and traditional basketball is that two balls are used and in play simultaneously, and players must use two baskets that are back-to-back. All basketball skills are used. After a basket has been made, the ball must be returned to the original start position before being thrown in again. Usually cones or mid-court lines designate this boundary.

Objects used:

Two basketballs

Organizational pattern:

Use two basketball courts that are placed back-to-back

Alternatives:

1. Use only one ball.
2. Permit shooting only from designated areas.
3. Add a Hula Hoop (hang it from the basket).

Create your own ideas!

What if . . .

Could you . . .

What would happen if . . .

Adapted Handball

Description:

The object of this game is for teams to score points. Designate one player to be a goalkeeper. The goalkeeper must remain seated in a chair or in a wheelchair at one end of the playing field. The player with the ball is not allowed to move; he or she must pass the ball to another teammate before moving to another location. If a player succeeds in passing the ball to his or her goalkeeper, the player who threw the ball changes places with the goalkeeper and the team gets one point. Then the other team starts with the ball. Players who do not have the ball are free to move around into new positions and to interfere with the other players' catching attempts. No physical contact is allowed, nor is the ball permitted to touch the floor. If either happens, the other team takes possession.

Objects used:

Ball, chair

Organizational pattern:

Two teams, randomly scattered about a playing area with goals at either end

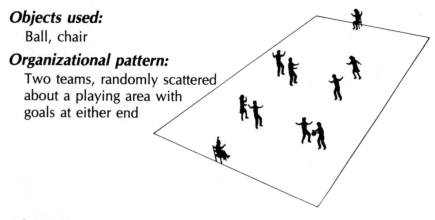

Alternatives:

1. Add a second ball.
2. Permit two dribbles before a pass.
3. Play for six minutes.

What if you had three teams playing one another?

Could you permit the goalkeeper to shoot a basket?

What would happen if you played this on scooters?

Contributed by: Erik Lindh—Norway

CHAPTER 7

NET GAMES

All games in this chapter require use of a net. In most cases, an object travels over or under the net. Each game challenges the players' abilities to receive and propel objects in some manner. Because reception and propulsion skills continue to be refined during childhood, it is important to consider the developmental status of players as the games take form. Using the activity design procedure, you will be able to alter a game's difficulty, thereby accommodating your developing players.

Many net games require players to contact (e.g., strike, deflect) a moving object with an implement such as a bat or racquet. Thus, you will notice that we suggest offering a wide variety of striking implements (for instance, varying in length, width, shape, weight) from which players may choose those to their liking. We also suggest modifying the height of a net, and its physical position in the playing area (e.g., slanted, stretched, or even twisted in the middle or covered with a blanket). Consider the advantages and disadvantages of these and other modifications as you proceed with these games.

Several of the games are adaptations of volleyball and tennis. Under-the-net games are also included. Some of the games are unique, particularly those contributed by our colleagues in Scandinavia. Some strategies are common to several of the net games, whereas others require distinctly different strategies from those familiar to many of us.

VOLLEYBALL GAMES

Keep It Going

Description:

The object of this game is for partners to keep the ball off the ground by using an overhead or forearm striking action. See if players can keep it going 10 seconds and how many times in a row they can keep it going.

Objects used:

A ball of your choice (e.g., Nerf ball, large balloon, beach ball, volleyball) for each pair

Organizational pattern:

Pairs randomly scattered about the gym

Alternatives:

1. Increase/decrease the degree of difficulty by changing the size or texture of the ball.
2. Increase the distance between both players.
3. Allow the ball to bounce on the floor only once.

What if you permitted players to hit the ball to themselves, thereby controlling it before sending it to their partners?

Could you add a net at shoulder height and hit the ball back and forth?

What would happen if you added a third and fourth player? Could players hit and move under the net to the other side and thus alternate the hitting responsibility?

Three Hits

Description:

The object of this game is for a team to score 15 points. The game is played like traditional volleyball except there is no service area and the ball must be hit three times on one side before going over the net. Only the serving team scores a point if the ball hits the ground on the opposing team's side. Hitting the net with any body part turns the ball over to the opposing team.

Objects used:

One ball of your choice—one that all can control, one net

Organizational pattern:

Two teams facing each other with a net at head level between them

Alternatives:

1. Raise or slant the net or cover it with a blanket so players cannot see the other team.

2. Permit only two hits or allow four or five hits.

3. Add a second ball.

What if you gradually increased the difficulty by changing the type of ball used?

Could you permit the ball to bounce once before a player hits it?

What would happen if you made this a cooperative game by totaling the number of successful hits over the net?

Four Corners Volleyball

Description:

The object of this game is for teams to have no balls in their quarter. Each team begins with one or two balls. Upon a go signal, each player uses volleyball skills to get the balls into the other teams' quarters. This is a cooperative game. See if players can keep the balls moving for three minutes.

Objects used:

Six to eight balls per game, two nets

Organizational pattern:

Four teams; one team in each quarter produced by crisscrossing two nets

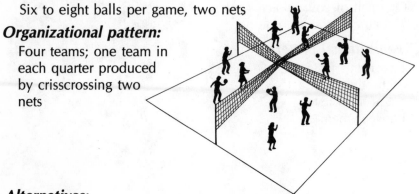

Alternatives:

1. Increase the number of balls.

2. Change the position of the nets.

3. Develop a point scoring system.

What if you awarded points that are variable with different ball types?

Could you see how long players could keep all of the balls in the air?

What would happen if everyone on a side had to hit the ball before sending it over the net?

Air Ball

Description:

The object of this game is for players to toss a ball over a net and land it on their opponent's mat, thus scoring a point. Each player may defend his or her mat using any part of the body to stop the ball. The first player to score 11 points wins.

Objects used:

A net, mats, and various kinds of balls

Organizational pattern:

One on one, each on a mat on either side of a net

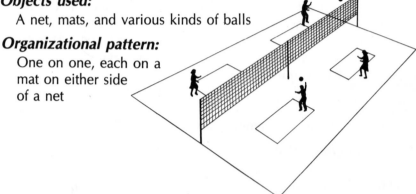

Alternatives:

1. Add a second mat to protect.

2. Increase the number of players on either side of the net.

3. Use different balls; change the net position.

What if you put able-bodied players on two mats and a handicapped player on one mat?

Could you change mat positions, thus decreasing target size?

What would happen if you had several nets at varying heights and permitted some players to hit at lower nets and others at only the higher nets? Could you have several players on each team and after each point rotate the players from one side of the net to the other?

TENNIS GAMES

Face to Face

Description:

Before playing Face to Face, players need to be able to perform these racquet skills: (a) hit the ball in the air to self, palm up, (b) hit the ball to self, palm down, (c) hit the ball to self, alternating palm up and down, (d) hit the ball to self, but switch racquet from one hand to the other on each hit, and (e) hit the ball three consecutive times, then hit the ball off the forehead onto the racquet. Upon a start signal, players select one of the preceding skills and see how many hits in a row they can make without missing.

Objects used:

Tennis racquets, Nerf tennis balls

Organizational pattern:

Each player with a racquet and ball scattered about the area

Alternatives:

1. Perform the skills while walking to a goal.
2. Change the racquet size or type of ball.
3. Bounce the ball off the floor or wall and play the same games.

> **What if** you made this a partner game and permitted players to bounce the ball on the floor before striking it with the racquet?
>
> **Could you** play this game off a wall, against targets on the wall, or hit the ball over wooden benches?
>
> **What would happen if** you played with teams of three or more players and added the total number of hits to get a score?

Contributed by: Halldor Skard—Oslo, Norway

Hit the Target

Description:

The object of this game is for players to use racquets to hit a ball over a net onto the wall, and keep it going for a specified time period or number of hits. Players should use forehand and backhand shots, refraining from using overhead shots.

Objects used:

Different types of striking implements (e.g., paddles, nylon racquets, tennis racquets), and a net or rope

Organizational pattern:

One or two players facing a wall; a net or rope at waist level between them and the wall

Alternatives:

1. Use a variety of balls (e.g., nylon balls, Nerf tennis balls, tennis balls).
2. Change the height of the net.
3. Increase the distance between the net and wall.

What if you placed a target on the wall?

Could you allow only volley shots over the net?

What would happen if you added a second net parallel to the first one?

Contributed by: Halldor Skard—Oslo, Norway

The Switch

Description:

This is a difficult cooperative game. The object is for four players to keep the ball in play while constantly switching positions. Using tennis skills, players strike the ball in a manner that permits opponents to return the shot. After hitting the ball over the net (1), the player slides to the right to receive the ball and return it over the net (2), jumps over the net to receive and return the ball (3), and moves to the right to receive and return ball (4). The cycle then continues.

Objects used:

Racquets, balls, a net or a rope

Organizational pattern:

Pairs facing one another, a net or rope at a low height everyone can jump over

Alternatives:

1. Change the net height.
2. Use only backhand strokes.

What if you created zones of play on either side of the net?

Could you gradually introduce traditional tennis rules?

What would happen if you played this game without players jumping over the net but retained the player switch rule?

Contributed by: Halldor Skard—Oslo, Norway

UNDER-THE-NET GAMES

Hit the Wall

Description:

The object of this game is for teams to roll balls under a net and hit the opposing team's wall. Players may use any body part to stop the balls, and may position themselves anywhere on their team's side of the net. Score one point each time the ball hits the wall—11 points wins.

Objects used:

Eight to twelve balls per team, one net

Organizational pattern:

Two teams facing each other, a net hanging between them so that a ball can be rolled beneath

Alternatives:

1. Use different size balls.
2. Increase the number of players per team.
3. Slant the net.

What if you gave each team only two minutes to hit the wall five times?

Could you change the players' body positions (e.g., sitting down)?

What would happen if you allowed only kicking the ball?

Contributed by: Inge Morisbak—Norway

Hit the Pin

Description:

The object of this game is for teams to score points by rolling a ball under the net and knocking over the other team's Indian clubs. One point is scored for each club knocked over. Players may stop the ball with any part of their bodies. It may be helpful to have some kind of a line at a set distance from the net, behind which players must stand to roll the ball. The first team to score three points wins.

Objects used:

Eight to twelve balls per team, one net, several Indian clubs or milk cartons

Organizational pattern:

Two teams facing one another, a net hanging between them so that a ball can be rolled beneath, and with Indian clubs or milk cartons in front of each team's back wall

Alternatives:

1. Decrease the number of balls.
2. Change body positions (e.g., sitting on the floor).
3. Score one point for the opponents every time a team knocks over one of its own pins.

What if you set a specific number of points that both teams were trying to prevent the other team from scoring?

Could you have players stand with their backs to the net and roll the ball through their legs?

What would happen if you added a player from the scoring team to the opponents' team each time a pin is knocked over?

Contributed by: Inge Morisbak—Norway

Ball to Ball

Description:

The object of this game is for teams to score points by making basketballs knock over Indian clubs (three points each) or by touching the wall behind the opposing team (one point). Play begins with both basketballs under the low net. To move the basketballs, players roll playground balls under the net so that they hit the basketballs. Players use only the lower body to stop oncoming balls. The first team to score seven points wins.

Objects used:

Two basketballs, many playground balls, Indian clubs or milk cartons, one net

Organizational pattern:

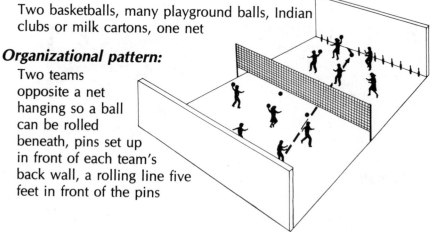

Two teams opposite a net hanging so a ball can be rolled beneath, pins set up in front of each team's back wall, a rolling line five feet in front of the pins

Alternatives:

Your chance to increase degree of difficulty of this game—consider objects, player, and limit categories.

Generate some additional games!

What if . . .

Could you . . .

What would happen if . . .

Contributed by: Inge Morisbak—Norway

All for You

Description:
The object of this game is for teams to have as many balls as possible on their opponents' side of the net. This is accomplished by rolling the balls under the net. Players use any body part to stop the balls, but must *always* remain seated. This is a fast-paced, high-action game.

Objects used:
Ten to twenty balls of all shapes and sizes, one net

Organizational pattern:
Two teams opposite one another, sitting on the floor on either side of the net

Alternatives:
1. Increase the number of balls.
2. Raise the net a little.
3. Decrease the number of players per team.

> **What if** you ask the players to redesign this game?
> **Could you** make this a cooperative game?
> **What would happen if** you allowed players to kick the ball?

Contributed by: Inge Morisbak—Norway

CHAPTER 8

ACTIVE ACADEMIC GAMES

These games are designed to supplement (not replace!) activities in academic areas such as language and mathematics. Each game entails specific academic operations and concepts. Why should you include these games? Because they include everyone regardless of ability, allow practice of academic skills, and incorporate movement. Besides, they are fun.

This type of activity is not new. Educators such as Bryant Cratty and James Humphrey popularized academic exercises coupled with movement activities in the 1960s and 1970s. Indeed, we've seen Cratty's *Active Learning* being used in many classrooms today.

The games contained in this chapter, however, differ from those just mentioned in one critical regard: Each is presented in the framework of modifying activities. Therefore, you will be able to create numerous variations from the few examples that we provide. We realize that many academic games can be created for a variety of subject matter areas. Our intent here is to provide you with some samples that represent how to modify academic games.

Memory Games

Short-term serial memory is a necessary skill for children to possess. Short-term memory is not only a prerequisite to other cognitive operations, but it is necessary for daily survival. Have you ever asked a young child to go to another classroom and get a ream of paper, a ruler, and three pencils? More often than not, the child returns with the paper and pencils, forgetting the ruler. Sometimes we teachers make some inappropriate remarks about the child's consciousness, unaware that perhaps the child's auditory short-term serial memory needs some work.

Serial memory can be enhanced. This section of the book addresses auditory and visual short-term serial memory. Like any other skill, memory strategies must be acquired and the skills *must* be practiced. Why not make this practice a fun movement activity? Common to all of these memory games are the following ideas:

- The difficulty levels of short-term serial memory activities can be increased or decreased.
- The more items to be remembered, the more difficult the task.
- The longer the delay between stimulus presentation and response, the greater the difficulty level.
- Requiring the children to attend to more than one stimulus form (e.g., auditory and visual) increases the difficulty of the task.

By employing these ideas, you can create a continuum of games that meets the needs of all of your students.

Sometimes we teachers wonder why our students cannot perform certain tasks we ask them to do. Have you ever given a series of instructions to your children in math or in an expressive language assignment only to discover, some 10 minutes later, that several children have not even begun? Maybe their auditory short-term memories are not capable of remembering "all that stuff you said." Reduce the number of instructions; monitor the responses by your children. In physical education classes, we use demonstration as a teaching strategy—this is, of course, heavily loaded with visual information that requires an adequate visual short-term memory. Might some children be unable to perform the whole task because their visual memory does not provide enough cues? Reduce the number of items that the children must selectively attend to and monitor the results.

In all of these games the movement tasks should reflect the children's current movement status. Use tasks everyone can do; the emphasis is on memory rather than specific movement skill development. Likewise, declaring winners is contraindicative to the purpose of the games. By employing a strategy that says, "Look around at your neighbors if you forget" (visual memory games), and "Ask your partner to restate the tasks" (auditory games) you are giving the children permission to share, help, and cooperate—is this not a part of the school experience we want to promote?

Math Games

Math is fun. Everyone can learn to enjoy using numbers. For many children, math time can be perplexing, but with the use of active math games, the concepts can be enjoyable. You, the teacher, can incorporate any math concept or operation into one of the following games—you can even design your own games.

Each of the following math games assumes a basic understanding of the math operation. The games are meant to provide opportunities for practicing math skills. Any type of movement can also be practiced in these games. Simply identify the skills you want the players to perform, match the difficulty level to each player's performance ability, and you will have accommodated each player—at least by game design. Is it also possible to accommodate the variety of academic levels found within any group of players? Some suggestions are offered that permit all abilities to play together at the same time.

Language Communication Games

We believe that you must be working on a specific academic skill in order to actually become competent with that skill. Consequently, language communication games and the other active academic games in this chapter are designed to use specific skills. A cluster of academic operations falls within the language communication category (e.g., symbol recognition and use, reading and all of its prerequisite skills, vocabulary building, and grammar). Active academic games can be designed to accommodate the many different reading strategies that currently exist. Most of the specialists agree that children must learn to read by attaching meaning to symbols, using a left-to-right visual scanning technique, and building vocabulary. By using the activity analysis strategies suggested in this book, it is possible to develop your own reading games. Just as we find most teachers placing children into different reading groups based upon reading ability, the same concept can be applied in relation to these games. However, it is also possible for most of the games to accommodate the continuum of reading abilities within the same game structure. This is accomplished by employing simple individualization strategies.

Let us now sample a few memory, math, and language communication games. Use the games as a guide and begin to develop your own academic games.

MEMORY GAMES

One Behind

Description:

The object of this visual short-term memory game is for players to copy the movements performed by the games leader. However, players must always remain one movement behind the games leader. For example, the leader performs movement A (hands on hips), and players memorize it, and when the leader performs movement B (hands on shoulders), the players perform movement A. Thus the players always remain one movement behind that performed by the leader. Play continues in this fashion. All locomotor, nonlocomotor, and fitness movements are permitted.

Objects used:

None

Organizational pattern:

Players randomly scattered directly in front of the games leader

Alternatives:

1. Change the sequence of the movements.

2. Increase/decrease the delay time between the movement presentation and the actual movement performance.

3. Use equipment (e.g., dribble a ball, jump rope).

> *What if* you used this game for fitness warm-ups (e.g., running in place, push-ups)?
>
> *Could you* play two moves behind? How about three moves behind?
>
> *What would happen if* you talked and demonstrated at the same time?

Couples Races

Description:

The object of this auditory short-term memory game is for players to remember all of the verbal instructions, perform all tasks properly, and return to the start position as soon as possible. Begin with only three tasks. For example, a player runs around his or her partner, touches an elbow to a knee, and jumps over the partner. The games leader gives movement tasks verbally to one partner of each pair of players. These tasks are to be performed in or around the partner's personal space. Do not name winners. The race is over when *everyone* is back and sitting down.

Objects used:

None are needed initially, but all small equipment can be used (e.g., balls, ropes, hoops)

Organizational pattern:

Two lines, partners opposite each other

Alternatives:

1. Increase the number of tasks.
2. Increase the amount of information within each task.
3. Decrease the delay time.

What if you added movements using manipulation of balls or ropes?

Could you give the players three tasks to perform and let them do them in any order?

What would happen if you always gave the players a specific "ending" task, such as sitting down or waving through their legs?

MATH GAMES

All 4s Circle Math

Description:

The object of this game is for players to respond accurately to a math question by jumping over everyone in their group and returning to the start position quickly. The game begins with each team member being assigned a number. The games leader gives each of the teams a math problem (e.g., 2 + 2 = _____). The player whose assigned number correctly answers the math problem gets up, jumps over everyone in the group, and returns to the start position.

Objects used:

None, or limited small equipment

Organizational pattern:

Teams of five to ten players lying on the floor in a circle, with heads toward the center of the circle

Alternatives:

1. Give everyone two numbers.
2. Alternate the position of players (e.g., on hands and knees; lying face up with feet in the center of the circle).
3. Weave around the players.

What if you used subtraction, multiplication, division, or other math functions?

Could you use fractions and/or negative numbers?

What would happen if you assigned players by ability grouping (some 2-digit, 3-digit subtraction abilities) and offer two different sets of problems each time?

The Number Grid

Description:

The object of the game is for players to accurately complete the team's multiplication sheet. Each team sends one player at a time to the grid. After throwing a bean bag onto the grid, the player uses the number the bag falls on to fill in the team's multiplication sheet. Sample score sheet:

8 × _____ =

9 × _____ =

4 × _____ =

Players put the number in the blank area, and return to their team by walking the length of a balance beam placed away from the groups. When all of the blanks have been completed, players perform the math operations as a team, and check their work.

Objects used:

Bean bags, balance beam, large number grid (can be made out of plastic painter's drop cloths or black lawn plastic and solid color contact paper or colored tape)

Organizational pattern:

Teams of five to ten players in a column relay pattern, facing the grid, one balance beam in a separate area

Alternatives:

1. Use other math operations.

2. Create other movement opportunities (e.g., skateboarding, unicycling, shooting baskets), and allow players to choose which movement to perform.

3. Have teams facing all sides of the grid.

LANGUAGE COMMUNICATION GAMES

Design a Letter

Description:
This is a very simple game designed to help young children recognize letters of the alphabet. Each group of players should move about the area with bean bags (they can be tossing them in the air, or balancing them on shoulders, heads, elbows). The group begins on a signal from the games leader—"Make the letter ____ with your bags." The first group to complete the task is the winner.

Objects used:
Bean bags

Organizational pattern:
Groups of five to eight players, randomly scattered, each with a bean bag

Alternatives:
1. Have players make letters without using equipment.
2. Make the tallest/smallest letter.
3. Use poles to shape the letters.

What if you asked players to perform different movements as they move about the area?

Could you use this game to make specific blending combinations?

What would happen if the groups had to work together to spell out words?

Contributed by: Ellen Haehre—Norway

Parts of Speech

Description:

The object of this game is for team members to accurately select the appropriate parts of speech. The games leader prints a paragraph from a previously read story on an 8½ × 11 sheet of paper and tapes the paper on a wall some distance from each team. Within each team, players become nouns, adjectives, or adverbs. Upon a start signal, the first player from each team goes to the paper by jumping rope, reads the paragraph, locates his or her part of speech, circles and codes it (n = noun, adj = adjective, v = verb). The player jumps rope back to the team, tags the next player, and goes to the end of the line and jumps into and out of a Hula Hoop five times. The game is played for four minutes. The games leader corrects the papers at the end of the game.

Objects used:

Hula Hoops, jump ropes, paragraph stories

Organizational pattern:

You choose—simply have teams of six to fifteen players—the fewer players per team, the less the waiting time

Alternatives:

1. Use other parts of speech (e.g., adverbs, prepositions).

2. Add other movements.

3. Vary distances traveled and organizational patterns used.

> **What if** you introduced foreign language vocabulary?
>
> **Could you** group players by ability and match the level of paragraph difficulty to each group?
>
> **What would happen if** each player had his or her own paragraph?

Homonym Game

Description:

The object of this game is for players to see how many pairs of homonyms their team can have at the end of the game. Upon a signal, the first player in each line jumps the rope six times, then moves to secure an accurate homonym pair (e.g., horse, hoarse). Upon locating a pair, the player moves to the basketball shooting area and has one opportunity to score a basket (which equals one point). The player returns to the team. When all pairs of cards are picked up, or when three minutes are up (whichever is first), the game is over. Count the number of pairs and add the number of baskets. The highest total wins.

Objects used:

Jump ropes, basketballs, homonym cards

Organizational pattern:

Spokes of a wheel—five to ten players in each line, homonym cards face up in center of pattern

Alternatives:

1. Increase the number of teams, thus decreasing waiting time.

2. Perform other movements.

3. Play the game with partners.

What if you made this a total point game?

Could you play this as a synonym game?

What would happen if all the cards were face down—would the game be more difficult?

SELECTED EXAMPLES OF TASK COMPLEXITY

Table A.1 Task Complexity: Kicking Factors

TC	Size object	Foot used	Weight of object	Type of kick	Movement of object	Shape of object
Easy	Large	Preferred	Light	Toe	Stationary	Round
↓						
Difficult	Small	Nonpreferred	Heavy	Instep	Fast	Oblong

Table A.2 Task Complexity: Catching Factors

TC	Object color	Angle of trajection	Object size	Object speed	Object weight	Object texture	Distance	Reception location
Easy	Blue	Horizontal	Large	Slow	Light	Soft	Near	Midline
↓	Yellow	Vertical	Medium	Fast	Medium	Firm	Medium	Preferred side
Difficult	White	Arc	Small	Faster	Heavy	Hard	Far	Nonpreferred side

Table A.3   Task Complexity: Jumping Factors

TC	Type of jump	Landing surface	Body position
Easy	Jump down	Crash pads Sawdust pit	Compact
	Horizontal jump	Gym mat	
Difficult	Vertical jump	Concrete surface	Extended

Table A.4   Task Complexity: Throwing Factors

TC	Object size	Object shape	Pattern used	Direction	Target movement
Easy	Small	Round	Overarm	Toward a wall	Stationary
	Medium	Oblong	Underarm	Toward a target, preferred side	Slightly moving
	Large	Irregular	Sidearm	Toward a target, nonpreferred side	Moving rapidly
Difficult					

Table A.5 Task Complexity: Striking Factors

TC	Object size	Object shape	Angle of trajection	Reception location	Object color/background color	Movement of object
Easy	Large	Round	Horizontal	Close to body	Blue/white	Stationary
	Medium	Oblong	Vertical	Preferred side	Yellow/white	Slow
Difficult	Small	Irregular	Arc	Nonpreferred side	White/white	Fast

Table A.6   Task Complexity: Strength Factors

TC	Weight	Duration	Distance/height
Easy	5 lbs	5 repetitions	100 yards/3 feet
		10 seconds	
		5 repetitions/15 seconds	
	10 lbs	10 repetitions	220 yards/6 feet
		20 seconds	
		10 repetitions/25 seconds	
Difficult	15 lbs	15 repetitions	440 yards/9 feet
		30 seconds	
		15 repetitions/40 seconds	

Table A.7   Task Complexity: Balance Factors

TC	Size of support base	Center of Gravity (C of G)	Speed	Time
Easy	Eight body parts	Directly over and close to the base of support	Slow	8 seconds
	Four body parts	Slightly off center and above base of support	Fast	18 seconds
Difficult	One body part	Moderately off center and far above the base of support	Faster	30 seconds

Table A.8 Task Complexity: Agility Factors

TC	Travel distance	Height	Direction change	Transition rhythm
Easy	Run, jump one foot, continue running	Jump over 6-inch-high object	One	Smooth
↓	Run, jump three feet, continue running	Jump over 1-foot-high object	Two	Irregular
Difficult	Run, jump five feet, continue running	Jump over 1½-foot-high object	Four	Rough

Table A.9 Task Complexity: Swinging/Swaying Factors

TC	Speed	Direction	Number of body parts	Level	External aids
Easy	Slow	One	Two	Medium	None
↓	Medium	Two	Three	Low	One
Difficult	Fast	Three	Four	High	Three

Table A.10   Task Complexity: Locomotor Factors—Even/Uneven-Beat Skills

TC	Level	Pathway	Direction	Time	Force	Flow	Relationship
Easy	Medium	Curved	Forward	Slow	Light	Free	Individual body within space
↓	High	Angular	Sideward	Medium	Medium	Jerky	Child-child Child-group
	Low	Zig zag	Backward	Fast	Heavy	Bound	Child-small equipment
Difficult							Child-large equipment

Table A.11   Task Complexity: Locomotor Factors—Rotary Motions

TC	Rhythm	Number/duration	End position	Speed	Starting position	Direction of movement	Body posture	Body parts contacting the surface
Easy	Smooth	One/short	Compact	Slow	Compact	Sideward	Compact	Many
↓								
Difficult	Irregular	Several/long	Extended	Fast	Extended	Backward	Extended	Few

REFERENCES

American Alliance for Health, Physical Education, Recreation and Dance. (1987). *AAHPERD Physical Best Test*. Reston, VA: Author.

Bandura, A. (1977). Self-efficacy: Toward a unifying theory of behavioral change. *Psychological Review, 84*, 191-215.

Bandura, A. (1981). Self-referent thought: A developmental analysis of self-efficacy. In J.H. Flavell & L. Ross (Eds.), *Social cognitive development* (pp. 200-239). New York: Cambridge University Press.

Cratty, B.J. (1976). *Active learning*. Englewood Cliffs, NJ: Prentice-Hall.

Dweck, C.S., & Elliott, E.S. (1984). Achievement motivation. In M. Hetherington (Ed.), *Social development: Carmichael's manual on child psychology* (pp. 643-691). New York: Wiley.

Eisen, G. (1988). *Children and play in the holocaust: Games among the shadows*. Amherst, MA: University of Massachusetts Press.

Griffin, N.S., & Keogh, J.F. (1981). Movement confidence and effective movement behavior in adapted physical education. *Motor skills: Theory into practice, 5*(1), 23-35.

Harter, S. (1983). Developmental perspectives on the self-system. In M. Hetherington (Ed.), *Social development: Carmichael's manual on child psychology* (pp. 275-385). New York: Wiley.

Hoffman, H., Young, J., & Klesius, S. (1981). *Meaningful movement for children*. Boston: Allyn & Bacon.

Humphrey, J. (1974). *Child learning*. Dubuque, IA: Brown.

Keogh, J.F., Griffin, N.S., & Spector, R. (1981). Observer perceptions of movement confidence. *Research Quarterly for Exercise and Sport, 52*(4), 465-473.

Magill, R.A. (1985). *Motor learning: Concepts and applications* (2nd ed.). Dubuque, IA: Brown.

Morris, G.S.D., & Stiehl, J. (1985). *Physical education: From intent to action*. Columbus, OH: Merrill.

Mosston, M., & Ashworth, S. (1986). *Teaching physical education* (3rd ed.). Columbus, OH: Merrill.

Orlick, T. (1978). *The cooperative sports and games book*. New York: Pantheon.

Schurr, E.L. (1980). *Movement experience for children: A humanistic approach to elementary school physical education* (3rd ed.). Englewood Cliffs, NJ: Prentice-Hall.

Torrance, E.P. (1969). *Creativity*. Belmont, CA: Dimensions.

Weiss, M. (1987). Self-esteem and achievement in children's sport and physical activity. In D. Gould & M.R. Weiss (Eds.), *Advances in pediatric sport sciences* (Vol. 2). Champaign, IL: Human Kinetics.

Weiss, M.R., Bredemeier, B.J., & Shewchuk, R.M. (1986). The dynamics of perceived competence, perceived control, and motivational orientation in youth sport. In M.R. Weiss & D. Gould (Eds.), *1984 Olympic Scientific Congress Proceedings: Vol. 10. Sport for children and youths* (pp. 89-101). Champaign, IL: Human Kinetics.